german conversation

DeMYSTiFieD

Demystified Series

Accounting Demystified
Advanced Calculus Demystified
Advanced Physics Demystified
Advanced Statistics Demystified
Algebra Demystified
Alternative Energy Demystified
American Sign Language Demystified
Anatomy Demystified
Astronomy Demystified
Audio Demystified
Biochemistry Demystified
Biology Demystified
Biotechnology Demystified
Business Calculus Demystified
Business Math Demystified
Business Statistics Demystified
C++ Demystified
Calculus Demystified
Chemistry Demystified
Circuit Analysis Demystified
College Algebra Demystified
Corporate Finance Demystified
Databases Demystified
Diabetes Demystified
Differential Equations Demystified
Digital Electronics Demystified
Earth Science Demystified
Electricity Demystified
Electronics Demystified
Engineering Statistics Demystified
English Grammar Demystified
Environmental Science Demystified
Everyday Math Demystified
Fertility Demystified
Financial Planning Demystified
Forensics Demystified
French Demystified
Genetics Demystified
Geometry Demystified
German Demystified
Global Warming and Climate Change Demystified
Hedge Funds Demystified
Investing Demystified
Italian Demystified
Japanese Demystified
Java Demystified
JavaScript Demystified
Latin Demystified
Lean Six Sigma Demystified
Linear Algebra Demystified
Macroeconomics Demystified
Management Accounting Demystified
Math Proofs Demystified
Math Word Problems Demystified
MATLAB ® Demystified
Medical Billing and Coding Demystified
Medical-Surgical Nursing Demystified
Medical Terminology Demystified
Meteorology Demystified
Microbiology Demystified
Microeconomics Demystified
Nanotechnology Demystified
Nurse Management Demystified
OOP Demystified
Options Demystified
Organic Chemistry Demystified
Pharmacology Demystified
Physics Demystified
Physiology Demystified
Pre-Algebra Demystified
Precalculus Demystified
Probability Demystified
Project Management Demystified
Psychology Demystified
Public Speaking and Presentations Demystified
Quantum Field Theory Demystified
Quantum Mechanics Demystified
Real Estate Math Demystified
Relativity Demystified
Robotics Demystified
Sales Management Demystified
Signals and Systems Demystified
Six Sigma Demystified
Spanish Demystified
Spanish Conversation Demystified
sql Demystified
Statics and Dynamics Demystified
Statistics Demystified
Technical Analysis Demystified
Technical Math Demystified
Trigonometry Demystified
Vitamins and Minerals Demystified

german conversation DeMYSTiFieD

Ed Swick

New York Chicago San Francisco Lisbon London Madrid Mexico City
Milan New Delhi San Juan Seoul Singapore Sydney Toronto

The McGraw-Hill Companies

1 2 3 4 5 6 7 8 9 10 11 12 13 14 15 16 17 18 19 20 21 WFR/WFR 0 9

ISBN 978-0-07-162722-1 (book and CD)
MHID 0-07-162722-7 (book and CD)

ISBN 978-0-07-162719-1 (book alone)
MHID 0-07-162719-7 (book alone)

Library of Congress Control Number 2009925528

Acknowledgment
With much gratitude to Stefan Feyen for all his help and suggestions.

McGraw-Hill books are available at special quantity discounts to use as premiums and sales promotions or for use in corporate training programs. To contact a representative, please e-mail us at bulksales@mcgraw-hill.com.

To Riane, AJ, Jalyn, Tori, and Riley, my terrific grandkids.

CONTENTS

INTRODUCTION

As the title suggests, *German Conversation Demystified* is not a grammar book. Refer to our companion book, *German Demystified*, for details on all aspects of German grammar. But use this unique book to develop your conversational skills and to increase your German vocabulary.

On occasion in each chapter, you will find a reference to a basic grammar point that is essential for understanding the conversational material. However, for the most part, this book is dedicated to providing you with phrases and structures useful in becoming conversant in your new language.

Various kinds of sentences are the vehicles for illustrating how a particular structure or group of vocabulary words is used. They are not presented at random or in an isolated form. Instead, they appear in related groups and in patterns that help to identify how they can be used by you.

Dialogues

Each chapter begins with a dialogue between two people. Their conversation introduces you to the general topic of the chapter and provides you with language that is natural and normal in contemporary Germany without being overwhelming. Practice saying the dialogues out loud. Study what they mean and how the words are used. Then answer the simple questions that follow to check your comprehension before going on to the next section of the chapter.

Pattern Sentences

You will be asked to repeat pattern sentences as you simultaneously see their English meanings. This is the introduction to the new structures and words of the chapter. These pattern sentences are then used to form drills, by means of which you can practice the important aspects of the sentences. And further drills will give you the opportunity to *create* new phrases based upon the pattern sentences you have practiced. The dialogues, pattern sentences, and many of the drills are on the accompanying CD. Use the CD tracks to hear correct pronunciation and the correct responses in the drills.

Additional Material

Some of the material in the chapters is not directly linked to the conversational target of that chapter. Instead, the purpose is to give you a breather from the rigors of spoken practice. For example, sidebars such as Culture Demystified provide you with cultural information not necessarily related to the pattern sentences and drills given in that section. Instead, in such a sidebar you learn how Germans relate to one another in their own special way, how their language makes them different from other people, or how they view the world around them.

There are Written Practice sections in each chapter that permit you to show in a brief writing drill that you comprehend the basic usage of a specific pattern. In addition, in some written practices you will encounter a dialogue similar to the one that introduces Chapters 2–15. But the sequence of the lines of dialogue is out of order. You will be asked to put the lines in the correct order as a check of your understanding of the content of the dialogue. The correct answers for these brief written practices are at the end of this book in the Answer Key.

A small but rather significant addition to each chapter is called "Phrases for Survival." In this paragraph you will encounter words and phrases critical for getting around the German-speaking world comfortably.

Quizzes and Tests

Each chapter ends with an open-book quiz with five multiple-choice questions and five sentence composition questions that review the concepts introduced in that chapter. You should try to achieve a score of eight correct out of ten on the chapter quiz before moving on to the next chapter.

This book is divided into three parts. The first two main parts are followed by a test with twenty-five questions that review the contents of the chapters within those parts. These tests are closed-book tests, and you should try to get a score of 75 percent before moving on to the next part. These tests are meant to be a measuring device to help you understand how well you have learned the conversational content of the chapters in each part. Following Part Three, after Chapter 15, there is then the Final Exam, which you can use as a culminating measuring device. The Final Exam stresses the information in the last five chapters but also includes aspects of the content from the first ten chapters. All the tests with the test questions and their correct answers are on your CD.

This book is intentionally called *German Conversation Demystified.* Use it as it is designed to be used: to learn to *speak* German. Don't *think* the phrases or just come up with answers in your mind. Speak out loud in a full voice. And if you stumble, say the phrase again. Imitate the native voices on the CD, and strive to perfect your accent and speed of delivery. With regular practice, the mystery of spoken German will soon be revealed to you.

PART ONE

CONVERSATION BASICS

CHAPTER 1

German Pronunciation

In this chapter you will learn:

The German Alphabet

German Pronunciation

Special Characters

Consonant Combinations

Vowel Combinations

Short and Long Vowels

The German Alphabet

The German alphabet is derived from the Latin alphabet just as English is. Although the letters are the same in both languages, German has its own pronunciation for some of them.

TRACK 1

Listen to the CD that accompanies this book to hear each letter pronounced and to hear a sample word that contains that letter. After you hear the letter or the sample word, always press "pause" and repeat what you hear.

Letter	Name	Example Word	English Meaning
Aa	ah	las	*read (past tense)*
Bb	bay	Boot	*boat*
Cc	tsay	Cent	*cent*
Dd	day	dann	*then*
Ee	ay	Tee	*tea*
Ff	eff	finden	*to find*
Gg	gay	geben	*to give*
Hh	hah	Haus	*house*
Ii	ee	Igel	*hedgehog*
Jj	yawt	ja	*yes*
Kk	kah	kalt	*cold*
Ll	ell	Laus	*louse*
Mm	emm	Maus	*mouse*
Nn	enn	nein	*no*
Oo	oh	oder	*or*
Pp	pay	parken	*to park*
Qq	koo	Quark	*curd cheese*
Rr	air	Ruhm	*fame*
Ss	ess	Sessel	*armchair*
Tt	tay	Teil	*part*
Uu	oo	U-Bahn	*subway*
Vv	fow	Volkswagen	*Volkswagen*
Ww	vay	wild	*wild*
Xx	ix	Taxi	*taxi*
Yy	uepsilon	physisch	*physical*
Zz	tset	Zelt	*tent*

Oral Practice 1-1

Say each word out loud. Look at the pronunciation on the right to check your accuracy.

German	English	Pronunciation
fett	*fat*	fett
so	*so*	zoh
Mann	*man*	munn
essen	*to eat*	es-sen
Mutter	*mother*	moo-tuh
Berlin	*Berlin*	bare-leen
sitzen	*to sit*	sit-zen
kennen	*to know*	ken-nen
Gabel	*fork*	gah-bel
hinter	*behind*	hin-tuh
Insel	*island*	in-zel
wiegen	*to weigh*	vee-ghen
Wagen	*car*	vah-ghen
jung	*young*	yoong
Zeh	*toe*	tsay
Zimmer	*room*	tsim-muh
Donner	*thunder*	dawn-uh
Tanne	*fir tree*	tun-neh
Tante	*aunt*	tahn-teh
links	*left*	linx
rot	*red*	rote
Ufer	*shore*	oo-fuh
gut	*good*	goot
alles	*everything*	uh-less
Name	*name*	nah-meh

German Pronunciation

The German language has special characters and letter combinations that are pronounced in their own way. Some are similar to English sounds, and others have a completely unique pronunciation.

SPECIAL CHARACTERS

Three German vowels often have an umlaut over them. These dots indicate a shift in the normal pronunciation of the letters.

Ää is very similar to the German letter **Ee**, which was illustrated previously; **Ää** is pronounced *ay*. For example:

Käse	*cheese*	k**ay**-zeh

Öö has a vowel sound that does not occur in English. It is similar to the vowel **e** in the English word *her*, but the final *r* sound is not voiced.

schön	*nice*	sh**er**n

Üü is pronounced like the sound **oo** with the lips tightly pursed, but the voice is saying **ee**. This same pronunciation is used with the German letter **Yy**.

Tür	*door*	**tuer**
System	*system*	z**ue**ss-tame

German also has a special consonant combination that does not exist in English. It is the combination of a German **s** and a **z** and is pronounced like a double **s** (**ss**). It replaces a double **s** after long vowel sounds or diphthongs. Its name is **ess-tset**, and it looks like this: **ß**.

weiß	*white*	vice
Gruß	*greeting*	grooss

When the letters **b**, **g**, and **d** end a word in German, they are pronounced **p**, **k**, and **t**, respectively. For example:

gel**b**	*yellow*	ghel**p**
hal**b**	*half*	hul**p**
Flu**g**	*flight*	floo**k**
klu**g**	*intelligent*	kloo**k**
Pfun**d**	*pound*	pfoon**t**
run**d**	*round*	roon**t**

Oral Practice 1-2

TRACK 2

Listen to the CD to hear a sample word that contains some unique letters. After you hear each sample word, press "pause" and repeat what you hear.

Sample Word	English	Sample Word	English
älter	*older*	Grüße	*greetings*
fällt	*falls*	Kasse	*cashier*
löst	*solves*	Flugzeug	*airplane*
böse	*angry*	Feld	*field*
Flüsse	*rivers*	aß	*ate*
klug	*smart*	Korb	*basket*
lügen	*to lie*	lag	*lay*
groß	*big*		

CONSONANT COMBINATIONS

A few consonant combinations are identical in both English and German. Some combinations, however, have their own unique pronunciation in German.

1. **Ch** stands for the sound of the friction of air at the back of the throat much like the *ch* sound in the Scottish word *loch*. For example: **ich** means *I* and is pronounced **ee*ch***. The italicized consonants ***ch*** will stand for this sound.
2. **Chs** in the middle of a word is pronounced like the English *x*. For example, **Sachsen** means *Saxony* and is pronounced **zahx-en**.
3. **Ck** is also pronounced like the English *ck*. For example, **schicken** means *to send* and is pronounced **shick-en**.
4. **H** that follows a vowel at the end of a syllable is not pronounced. For example, **gehen** means *to go* and is pronounced **gay-en**.
5. With **pf**, both the **p** and the **f** are sounded in the pronunciation. For example, **pfiff** means *whistled* and is pronounced **pfiff**.
6. **Sch** is like the English combination *sh*. For example: **Schule** means *school* and is pronounced **shoo-leh**.
7. Two consonant combinations—**sp** and **st**—add the sound **sh** to their pronunciation. For example, **Sport** means *sports* and is pronounced **shport**. **Still** means *quiet* and is pronounced **shtill**.

8. **Th** exists in German, but it is pronounced like a **t**. For example, the German noun **Theater** means *theater*, but it is pronounced **tay-ah-tuh**.
9. **Tsch** sounds like the English combination *ch*. For example, **Tschechien** means *Czech Republic* and is pronounced **chech-ee-en**.
10. **Tz** is pronounced as it would be in English. For example, **letzte** means *last* and is pronounced **letz-teh**.

VOWEL COMBINATIONS

The following vowel combinations stand for a single sound but, in most cases, have a sound different from a single vowel:

1. **Aa** is pronounced as a long **ah**. For example, **Haar** means *hair* and is pronounced **hahr**.
2. **Au** is pronounced together as **ow**. For example, **kaufen** means *to buy* and is pronounced **cow-fen**.
3. **Äu** is pronounced **oi**. For example, **Fräulein** means *Miss* and is pronounced **froi-line**.
4. **Ee** has a long **ay** sound. For example, **Tee** means *tea* and is pronounced **tay**.
5. **Ei** is pronounced **eye**. For example, **mein** means *my* and is pronounced **mine**.
6. **Eu** is also pronounced **oi**. For example, **Freude** means *joy* and is pronounced **froi-deh**.
7. **Ie** is pronounced **ee**. For example, **sieht** means *sees* and is pronounced **zeet**.
8. **Oo** has a long **oh** sound. For example, **Boot** means *boat* and is pronounced **bote**.

Oral Practice 1-3

Listen to your CD to hear the pronunciation of words with special consonant or vowel combinations. After each word, press "pause" and repeat what you hear.

German	**English**	**German**	**English**
sprechen	*to speak*	Eule	*owl*
Stadt	*city*	teilen	*to share*

German	English	German	English
setzen	*to set*	schrieb	*wrote*
schrecken	*to scare*	Kaufmann	*businessman*
Thema	*topic*	Seemann	*seaman*
Tisch	*table*	Säule	*column*
Käfig	*cage*	fährt	*drives*
sehen	*to see*	Paar	*pair*
Pförtner	*doorman*	Freundin	*girlfriend*
sechs	*six*	Boote	*boats*

SHORT AND LONG VOWELS

Vowels tend to be pronounced short before a double consonant and long before a single consonant or a consonant preceded by **h**. Let's look at some examples:

Long Vowel			Short Vowel		
lasen	(lah-zen)	*read*	lassen	(luhs-sen)	*to let*
stehlen	(shtay-len)	*to steal*	stellen	(shtel-len)	*to put*
gib	(geep)	*gives*	Mitte	(mit-teh)	*middle*
Hof	(hohf)	*courtyard*	hoffen	(hawf-fen)	*to hope*
tun	(toon)	*to do*	Suppe	(zoop-peh)	*soup*

VOCABULARY DEMYSTIFIED

The German Vowel *U*

English speakers tend to use the long *oo* sound for all words that have the vowel **u** in German. But the short and long **oo** sounds must be distinguished in German. In English that vowel combination has two pronunciations as well. For example, long *oo—moon, soon*; and short *oo-look, shook*. Be sure to use the appropriate **oo** in German: **tun** (long **oo**); **Suppe** (short **oo**).

Oral Practice 1-4

TRACK 4

Listen to your CD to hear the pronunciation of words with long or short vowel sounds. After each word, press "pause" and repeat what you hear.

German	English	German	English
stören	*to disturb*	gelb	*yellow*
gelacht	*laughed*	Band	*ribbon*
Kaffee	*coffee*	verlassen	*to leave*
Brötchen	*roll*	fluchen	*to curse*
Schlange	*snake*	küssen	*to kiss*
jünger	*younger*	besser	*better*
floh	*fled*	gibt	*gives*
Sprüche	*sayings*		

QUIZ

Listen to your CD to hear five words. Press "pause" to repeat each one as you hear it. Decide whether the word contains an **ess-tset** (**ß**) or a double **s** (**ss**). Then listen to the correct answer on your CD.

1. **ß** or **ss**
2. **ß** or **ss**
3. **ß** or **ss**
4. **ß** or **ss**
5. **ß** or **ss**

Listen to your CD to hear five words. Press "pause" to repeat each word. Decide whether the word contains a long or a short vowel sound. Then listen to the correct answer on the CD.

6. long/short vowel sound
7. long/short vowel sound
8. long/short vowel sound
9. long/short vowel sound
10. long/short vowel sound

CHAPTER 2

Talking About People and Things

In this chapter you will learn:

Greeting People: Grüße und Begrüßungen

Names and Titles

Asking How Someone Is

Asking Wer ist das? *(Who is that?) and* Was ist das*? (What is that?)*

Greeting People: *Grüße und Begrüßungen*

 TRACK 6

Listen to the following dialogue on your CD. After you hear a phrase or sentence on a track, always press "pause" and repeat what you hear.

SABINE: Guten Tag, Erik.	*Hello, Erik.*
ERIK: Guten Tag, Sabine. Wie geht's?	*Hello, Sabine. How are you?*
SABINE: Gut, danke. Und dir?	*Fine, thanks. And you?*
ERIK: Nicht schlecht. Wer ist das?	*Not bad. Who is that?*
SABINE: Das ist der neue Professor.	*That is the new professor.*
ERIK: Wie heißt er?	*What is his name?*
SABINE: Wagner. Professor Otto Wagner.	*Wagner. Professor Otto Wagner.*
ERIK: Auf Wiedersehen, Sabine.	*Good-bye, Sabine.*
SABINE: Tschüs, Erik.	*So long, Erik.*

Dialogue Review

Answer the following questions about the dialogue **Grüße und Begrüßungen** out loud. Cover the correct answers shown on the right. Use them to compare with your own answers.

1. Wie geht es Erik? *How is Erik?*	Es geht Erik nicht schlecht.
2. Wie heißt der neue Professor? *What is the new professor's name?*	Der neue Professor heißt Otto Wagner.

NAMES AND TITLES

When asking someone's name, use the phrase **Wie heißt er?** for a male and **Wie heißt sie?** for a female (*What is his name?/What is her name?*). Some traditional German names are:

Für Jungen *For Boys*	**Für Mädchen** *For Girls*
Gerhardt	Charlotte
Reinhardt	Gretchen
Helmut	Ingrid
Otto	Frieda
Werner	Waltraud

Just like in the United States, in the German-speaking world there are names that come from different cultures, many of which are in vogue today. Sometimes, however, their popularity is often fleeting and new names soon become the latest trend. Some contemporary names still in use are:

Für Jungen *For Boys*	**Für Mädchen** *For Girls*
Erik	Gudrun
Boris	Tanja
Christoph	Natascha
Felix	Angela
Nils	Iris

If you are on a formal basis with someone and use the person's last name, be sure to use the appropriate title:

Herr	*Mr.*
Frau	*Mrs., Ms., Miss*
Professor	*Professor (male or female)*
Doktor	*Dr. (male or female)*

When you say hello to someone, use the person's first name in an informal situation. Use the person's title and last name in a formal situation. For example:

Guten Tag, Felix.	*Hello, Felix.*
Guten Tag, Angela.	*Hello, Angela.*

Guten Tag, Herr Braun. *Hello, Mr. Brown.*

Guten Tag, Frau Keller. *Hello, Ms. Keller.*

The expression **Guten Tag** literally means *good day*. It's the general way of saying *hello* in the middle of the day. In the morning you say **Guten Morgen** (*good morning*), and in the evening you say **Guten Abend** (*good evening*). When it's late or you're going to bed, say **Gute Nacht** (*good night*). Practice saying these four expressions out loud:

Guten Morgen, Doktor Schmidt. *Good morning, Dr. Schmidt.*

Guten Tag, Frau Keller. *Good day, Ms. Keller.*

Guten Abend, Angelika. *Good evening, Angelika.*

Gute Nacht, Herr Schneider. *Good night, Mr. Schneider.*

Oral Practice 2-1

TRACK 7

Look at the following names and the times of day provided in parentheses, and say hello to that person with the appropriate greeting for that time of day. Listen to your CD for the correct answers. After you hear a phrase or sentence on a track, always press "pause" and repeat what you hear.

Erik (morning)

Herr Benz (evening)

Frau Bauer (night)

Ingrid (afternoon)

Professor Schneider (morning)

ASKING HOW SOMEONE IS

To ask how someone is in German, say **Wie geht's?** The following are a few typical responses. Notice the plus signs accompanying the responses. They tell you how positive the response is. You'll use plus signs as signals for your own responses in the next oral practice.

Sehr gut, danke. (++++)	*Very well, thanks.*
Gut, danke. Und dir? (+++)	*Fine, thanks. And you?*
Nicht schlecht. (++)	*Not bad.*
Nicht so gut. (+)	*Not so well.*

Oral Practice 2-2

TRACK 8

Look at each name provided and ask the person how he or she is. Then, based upon the number of plus signs shown, give the person's likely response to your question. Listen to the CD for correct answers. For example:

Erik ++++
You say: Wie geht's, Erik? *Likely response*: Gut, danke. Und dir?

Luise +++

Otto +

Angela ++++

Gerhardt ++

Sabine +++

Tanja ++++

Herr Bauer +

Frau Schneider ++

Asking *Wer ist das?* (Who is that?) and *Was ist das?* (What is that?)

To ask who someone is, say **Wer ist das?** (*Who is that?*) The response begins with **Das ist ...** (*That is . . .*). To ask what something is, say **Was ist das?** (*What is that?*) Once again, begin the response with **Das ist ...** .

Person or Object	Question	Answer
der Professor	Wer ist das?	Das ist der Professor.
Frau Bauer	Wer ist das?	Das ist Frau Bauer.
die Schule (*school*)	Was ist das?	Das ist die Schule.
das Haus (*house*)	Was ist das?	Das ist das Haus.

GRAMMAR DEMYSTIFIED

Definite Articles

There are three words in German for *the*: **der**, which refers to masculine nouns; **die**, which refers to feminine nouns; and **das**, which refers to neuter nouns.

der Doktor	*the doctor*
die Frau	*the woman*
das Buch	*the book*

German gender rules are not based exclusively on sexual gender. Some nouns that refer to people can be neuter. And some objects can be masculine or feminine nouns. For example:

das Kind	*child*
das Mädchen	*girl*
der Stuhl	*chair*
der Wagen	*car*
die Lampe	*lamp*
die Bluse	*blouse*

Written Practice 2-1

The following is a list of animate and inanimate nouns. If the noun is animate, write the question **Wer ist das?** and give the appropriate response. If it is inanimate, ask the question **Was ist das?** and give the appropriate response. For example:

Erik *Wer ist das? Das ist Erik.*

1. Sabine ______
2. der Professor ______
3. der Stuhl ______
4. die Schule ______
5. das Kind ______
6. das Haus ______
7. die Lampe ______
8. Frau Benz ______
9. Angela ______
10. der Wagen ______

Study the following list of new vocabulary words. Each one is used in a sentence saying *that is the person/thing*. Look at each word and sentence carefully; then go on to the Oral Practice that follows.

der Wagen *car*	Das ist der Wagen.	*That is the car.*
der Mann *man*	Das ist der Mann.	
die Lehrerin *female teacher*	Das ist die Lehrerin.	
die Jacke *jacket*	Das ist die Jacke.	
der Tourist *tourist*	Das ist der Tourist.	
das Brot *bread*	Das ist das Brot.	
das Glas *glass*	Das ist das Glas.	
der Apfel *apple*	Das ist der Apfel.	
der Kuchen *cake*	Das ist der Kuchen.	

Oral Practice 2-3

TRACK 9

Using the list of nouns as your cues, ask either *who that is* or *what that is*, and then answer the question. Listen to your CD to hear the correct answers. After you hear a phrase or sentence on a track, always press "pause" and repeat what you hear.

apple

female teacher

jacket

cake

bread

tourist

glass

man

child

school

VOCABULARY DEMYSTIFIED

Using Titles

To address a person with a title without using his or her last name, place **Herr** or **Frau** before the title. For example:

Guten Tag, Herr Doktor./Guten Tag, Frau Doktor.	*Hello, doctor.*
Guten Abend, Herr Professor./Guten Abend, Frau Professor.	*Hello, professor.*

Written Practice 2-2

The following lines of dialogue are out of sequence. Place a number, from 1 to 8, in each blank to show the appropriate order for the lines.

_____ Auf Wiedersehen, Frau Keller.

_____ Wer ist das, Felix?

_____ Das ist die Lehrerin.

_____ Sie heißt Frau Bauer.

_____ Guten Tag, Felix.

_____ Auf Wiedersehen, Felix.

_____ Wie heißt sie?

_____ Guten Tag, Frau Keller.

PHRASES FOR SURVIVAL

Getting a Name Right

Add these useful phrases to your language arsenal to help you get by in the German-speaking world:

Hallo!	*Hi!*
Wie heißen Sie?	*What is your name?*
Ich heiße Brown. Thomas Brown.	*My name is Brown. Thomas Brown.*

QUIZ

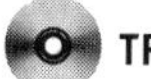

TRACK 10

Responding to questions. Listen to your CD to hear each question. Press "pause" to repeat the question out loud and select your answer—a, b, or c. Then listen to the correct answer on the CD, making sure to repeat what you hear.

1. (a) der Lehrer
   (b) Gut, danke.
   (c) Frau Bauer

2. (a) Erik
   (b) Frau Schneider
   (c) Sabine

3. (a) Das ist Herr Braun.
   (b) Das ist die Lehrerin.
   (c) Das ist die Bluse.

4. (a) Nicht so gut.
   (b) die Schule
   (c) Das ist das Glas.

5. (a) Das ist das Brot.
   (b) Das ist die Jacke.
   (c) Das ist der Tourist.

Using each noun as your cue, ask either *who that is* or *what that is*. Then answer the question appropriately. Listen to the correct answers on your CD, making sure to repeat what you hear.

6. apple
7. female teacher
8. man

Say *hello* appropriately for the time of day indicated by the cue. Listen to the correct answers on your CD, making sure to repeat what you hear.

9. morning
10. evening

CHAPTER 3

Asking Questions

In this chapter you will learn:

Asking Was machst du? *(What are you doing?)*

Forming Yes/No Questions

Negation with Nicht

Asking *Was machst du*? (What are you doing?)

TRACK 11

Listen to the following dialogue on your CD. After you hear a phrase or sentence on a track, always press "pause" and repeat what you hear.

THOMAS: Hallo, Astrid! Wie geht's?	*Hi, Astrid! How are you?*
ASTRID: Ganz gut. Was machst du jetzt?	*Quite well. What are you doing now?*

THOMAS: Ich gehe nach Hause. Und du?	*I am going home. And you?*
ASTRID: Ich gehe zur Bibliothek.	*I am going to the library.*
THOMAS: So spät?	*So late?*
ASTRID: Ja, ich muss lernen.	*Yes, I have to study.*
THOMAS: Wohnst du noch in der Hauptstraße?	*Are you still living on Main Street?*
ASTRID: Nein, nicht weit von hier.	*No, not far from here.*
THOMAS: Wo denn?	*Well, where?*
ASTRID: Beim Stadtpark.	*Near the city park.*
THOMAS: Wie schön!	*That is great!*

Dialogue Review

Answer the following questions about the dialogue **Was machst du?** out loud. Cover the correct answers shown on the right. Use them to compare with your own answers.

1. Wie geht es Astrid? *How is Astrid?*	Es geht Astrid ganz gut.
2. Geht Astrid nach Hause? *Is Astrid going home?*	Nein, Astrid geht zur Bibliothek.
3. Wo wohnt Astrid? *Where does Astrid live?*	Astrid wohnt beim Stadtpark.

Forming Yes/No Questions

Forming German questions is quite simple. If the question can be answered with **ja** or **nein** (*yes* or *no*), just place the verb in front of the subject and you have a question. Recite each of the following pairs of questions and their responses out loud:

Geht es Astrid ganz gut?	*Is Astrid feeling quite well?*
Ja, es geht Astrid ganz gut.	*Yes, Astrid is feeling quite well.*
Geht Thomas zur Bibliothek?	*Is Thomas going to the library?*
Nein, Thomas geht nicht zur Bibliothek.	*No, Thomas is not going to the library.*
Geht er nach Hause?	*Is he going home?*
Ja, er geht nach Hause.	*Yes, he is going home.*
Wohnt Astrid in der Hauptstraße?	*Does Astrid live on Main Street?*
Nein, Astrid wohnt nicht in der Hauptstraße.	*No, Astrid does not live on Main Street.*
Wohnt sie beim Stadtpark?	*Does she live near the city park?*
Ja, sie wohnt beim Stadtpark.	*Yes, she lives near the city park.*

GRAMMAR DEMYSTIFIED

Using *Geht*

The pronouns **er** and **sie** (*he* and *she*) can replace masculine and feminine nouns, respectively.

Thomas geht nach Hause.	**Er** geht nach Hause.
Astrid wohnt beim Stadtpark.	**Sie** wohnt beim Stadtpark.

Notice that **geht** is used in the expression that asks how someone is and that it is also a conjugation of the verb that means *to go*. In the expression **Wie geht's?** you are actually saying *How goes it?* That's how you say *How are you?* in German. **Geht's** in this instance is a contraction of **geht es**, formed in the same way as contractions in English.

TRACK 12

In the dialogue, Thomas is going home. But, of course, there are many other places he could be going. Listen to the following phrases of possible destinations on your CD. After you hear a phrase or sentence on a track, always press "pause" and repeat what you hear.

Thomas geht nach Hause.	*Thomas is going home.*
Thomas geht zur Bibliothek.	*Thomas is going to the library.*
Thomas geht zum Stadtpark.	*Thomas is going to the city park.*
Thomas geht zum Restaurant.	*Thomas is going to the restaurant.*
Thomas geht zur Schule.	*Thomas is going to the school.*
Thomas geht zur Party.	*Thomas is going to the party.*
Thomas geht zur Arbeit.	*Thomas is going to work.*
Thomas geht zum Bahnhof.	*Thomas is going to the train station.*

Note in the previous sentences that the word **zum** (*to the*) is used with masculine and neuter nouns. The word **zur** (*to the*) is used with feminine nouns. These are contractions of **zu dem** and **zu der** (*to the*), respectively.

Oral Practice 3-1

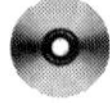 TRACK 13

Listen to the questions that ask *what he is doing* on your CD. Press "pause" and repeat each question out loud before responding by telling *where he is going* based upon the following words. Listen to the correct answers on your CD, making sure to repeat what you hear.

school

restaurant

city park

homeward

party

train station

work

library

Written Practice 3-1

Rewrite the following sentences as questions. For example:

Er geht nach Hause. Geht er nach Hause?

1. Er geht zum Stadtpark. ____________________?
2. Otto geht zur Schule. ____________________?
3. Astrid geht zur Party. ____________________?
4. Sie geht zum Bahnhof. ____________________?
5. Herr Keller geht zur Arbeit. ____________________?
6. Frau Bauer geht zum Restaurant. ____________________?
7. Das Kind geht zur Bibliothek. ____________________?
8. Professor Schneider geht nach Hause. ____________________?

Negation with *Nicht*

When you answer a question with **nein**, you can include the adverb **nicht** (*not*) in your response. For example:

Geht er nach Hause?	*Is he going home?*
Nein, er geht nicht nach Hause.	*No, he is not going home.*
Geht sie zur Schule?	*Does she go to school?*
Nein, sie geht nicht zur Schule.	*No, she does not go to school.*

This use of **nicht** for negation occurs with other verbs as well.

Wohnt Hans in Berlin?	*Does Hans live in Berlin?*
Nein, Hans wohnt nicht in Berlin.	*No, Hans does not live in Berlin.*
Ist das Frau Schneider?	*Is that Ms. Schneider?*
Nein, das ist nicht Frau Schneider.	*No, that is not Ms. Schneider.*

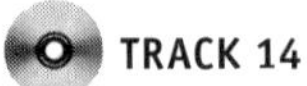 TRACK 14

Listen to the following questions on your CD. Press "pause" after each question to repeat what you hear. Then, in the negative, respond to the question. Cover the answers in the right-hand column and compare them with your own. For example:

Wohnt Frau Benz in Berlin?
You say: Nein, Frau Benz wohnt nicht in Berlin.

Geht Herr Braun zum Bahnhof?	Nein, Herr Braun geht nicht zum Bahnhof.
Wohnt Nils in Hamburg?	Nein, Nils wohnt nicht in Hamburg.
Ist er der Lehrer?	Nein, er ist nicht der Lehrer.
Arbeitet Astrid in der Bibliothek?	Nein, Astrid arbeitet nicht in der Bibliothek.
Geht Frau Bauer zum Stadtpark?	Nein, Frau Bauer geht nicht zum Stadtpark.
Wohnt er in Amerika?	Nein, er wohnt nicht in Amerika.
Ist das die Jacke?	Nein, das ist nicht die Jacke.
Arbeitet Erik in Berlin?	Nein, Erik arbeitet nicht in Berlin.
Wohnt sie in der Hauptstraße?	Nein, sie wohnt nicht in der Hauptstraße.
Ist der Tourist in Paris?	Nein, der Tourist ist nicht in Paris.

Oral Practice 3-2

Read each question out loud; then respond in both the positive and the negative. Cover the answers shown, and use them to compare with your own answers. For example:

Geht Hans nach Hause?
You say: Ja, Hans geht nach Hause. Nein, Hans geht nicht nach Hause.

Geht er zum Stadtpark?	Ja, er geht zum Stadtpark. Nein, er geht nicht zum Stadtpark.

Wohnt sie in Hamburg?	Ja, sie wohnt in Hamburg. Nein, sie wohnt nicht in Hamburg.
Arbeitet Sabine in der Bibliothek?	Ja, Sabine arbeitet in der Bibliothek. Nein, Sabine arbeitet nicht in der Bibliothek.
Ist Frau Benz Lehrerin?	Ja, Frau Benz ist Lehrerin. Nein, Frau Benz ist nicht Lehrerin.
Geht es Astrid gut?	Ja, es geht Astrid gut. Nein, es geht Astrid nicht gut.
Geht Professor Bauer zur Schule?	Ja, Professor Bauer geht zur Schule. Nein, Professor Bauer geht nicht zur Schule.
Wohnt Erik in Berlin?	Ja, Erik wohnt in Berlin. Nein, Erik wohnt nicht in Berlin.
Arbeitet Herr Braun in Amerika?	Ja, Herr Braun arbeitet in Amerika. Nein, Herr Braun arbeitet nicht in Amerika.
Ist die Jacke braun? (*brown*)	Ja, die Jacke ist braun. Nein, die Jacke ist nicht braun.
Geht es Frau Keller schlecht?	Ja, es geht Frau Keller schlecht. Nein, es geht Frau Keller nicht schlecht.

Written Practice 3-2

Fill in each blank with the missing verb: **geht**, **ist**, or **wohnt**.

1. Es ______________ Astrid ganz gut.
2. Er ______________ in der Hauptstraße.
3. Der Mann ______________ in der Bibliothek.
4. ______________ Frau Keller beim Stadtpark?
5. ______________ das Professor Schneider?

6. Das Kind _______________ zur Schule.
7. Herr Schäfer _______________ nicht der Lehrer.
8. _______________ die Jacke braun?
9. Pierre _______________ in Paris.
10. _______________ Erik jetzt nach Hause?

Written Practice 3-3

The following lines of dialogue are out of sequence. Place a number, from 1 to 9, in each blank to show the appropriate order for the lines.

_____ Sabine, wie geht's?

_____ Wie schön!

_____ Ganz gut. Was machst du jetzt?

_____ Hallo, Erik!

_____ Ich gehe zur Bibliothek.

_____ Nein, beim Stadtpark.

_____ Auf Wiedersehen, Erik.

_____ Tschüs, Sabine.

_____ Wohnst du noch beim Bahnhof?

VOCABULARY DEMYSTIFIED

The Preposition *Nach*

To say that you're going to a city or a country, use the preposition **nach** to mean *to*. For example:

Ich fahre nach Berlin.	*I am going to Berlin.*
Wir fahren nach München.	*We are going to Munich.*
Mein Freund reist nach England.	*My friend is traveling to England.*
Reisen Sie nach Amerika?	*Are you traveling to America?*

PHRASES FOR SURVIVAL

Finding an English Speaker

Add these useful phrases to your language arsenal to help you get by in the German-speaking world:

Sprechen Sie Englisch?	*Do you speak English?*
Spricht jemand hier Englisch?	*Does anyone here speak English?*
Danke schön.	*Thank you.*
Vielen Dank.	*Thanks a lot.*
Bitte schön.	*You're welcome.*

QUIZ

TRACK 15

Responding to questions. Listen to your CD to hear each question. Press "pause" to repeat the question out loud and select your answer—a, b, or c. Then listen to the correct answer on the CD, making sure to repeat what you hear.

1. (a) Nein, zum Bahnhof.
   (b) Guten Abend.
   (c) Nein, in Hamburg.

2. (a) Nein, es geht Astrid gut.
   (b) Ja, sie ist Lehrerin.
   (c) Ja, ganz gut.

3. (a) Ja, er geht zum Bahnhof.
   (b) Nein, er geht zur Party.
   (c) Ja, er ist in Amerika.

4. (a) Nein, in der Hauptstraße.
   (b) Ja, nach Hause.
   (c) Ja, er wohnt beim Bahnhof.

5. (a) Nein, er geht nicht zur Bibliothek.
   (b) Ganz gut.
   (c) Ja, sie geht zum Stadtpark.

Using the pair of the nouns provided as your cue, ask whether the person is going to the destination. Listen to the correct answer on the CD, making sure to repeat what you hear.

6. das Kind, Schule
7. das Mädchen, Party
8. Frau Schneider, Restaurant
9. er, Bibliothek
10. der Tourist, nach Hause

CHAPTER 4

Going Places

In this chapter you will learn:

Gehen wir einkaufen! *Let's go shopping!*

Asking Questions with Haben

Asking Questions with Sein

Asking Where Someone Is Traveling Using Wo *and* Wohin

Gehen wir einkaufen! Let's go shopping!

TRACK 17

Listen to the following dialogue on your CD. After you hear a phrase or sentence on a track, always press "pause" and repeat what you hear.

RENATE: Wie geht's, Dirk? — *How are you, Dirk?*

DIRK: Es geht. Renate, hast du heute nachmittag Zeit? — *I am all right. Renate, do you have some time this afternoon?*

RENATE: Warum denn? — *Why?*

DIRK: Ich möchte einkaufen gehen. Ich brauche eine neue Jacke. — *I would like to go shopping. I need a new jacket.*

RENATE: Ich will auch einkaufen gehen. Aber ich habe nur zehn Euro. — *I want to go shopping, too. But I have only ten euros.*

DIRK: Kein Problem. Ich leihe dir einen Zwanziger. Gehen wir um elf ins Einkaufszentrum! — *No problem. I will loan you a twenty. Let's go to the mall at eleven!*

RENATE: Schön. Wo ist dein Bruder? Kommt er mit? — *Great. Where is your brother? Is he coming along?*

DIRK: Nein, er hat morgen eine Prüfung. — *No, he has a test tomorrow.*

RENATE: Na, gut. Bis später, Dirk. — *Oh, OK. See you later, Dirk.*

DIRK: Auf Wiederhören! — *Good-bye!*

Dialogue Review

Answer the following questions about the dialogue **Gehen wir einkaufen!** out loud. Cover the correct answers shown on the right. Use them to compare with your own answers.

1. Was möchte Dirk tun? — Dirk möchte einkaufen gehen.
   What would Dirk like to do?

2. Wie viele Euro hat Renate? — Sie hat nur zehn Euro.
   How many euros does Renate have?

3. Kommt Dirks Bruder mit? — Nein, Dirks Bruder kommt nicht mit.
   Is Dirk's brother coming along?

GRAMMAR DEMYSTIFIED

Pronouns

Just like English, German has a variety of pronouns. But there is a slight difference in the German second person pronoun: the pronoun *you* has three forms. **Du** is the singular form of *you* and is used informally with children, family members, or close friends. **Ihr** is the plural form of **du**. And **Sie** (always with a capital **S**) is the formal singular or formal plural form and is used with strangers, people of authority, or as a means of showing respect or courtesy.

Singular	**Plural**	
du	ihr	*(informal)*
Sie	Sie	*(formal)*

Many of the verbs in the previous dialogue are in the present tense. Note that German has different verb endings for the various persons. Let's look at a few verb conjugations with all the pronouns. Notice how the endings are consistent from one verb to another.

Pronoun	**gehen**	**brauchen**	**kaufen**	**kommen**	(*to go*; *to need*; *to buy*; *to come*)
ich *I*	gehe	brauche	kaufe	komme	(*I go*; *I need*; *I buy*; *I come*)
du *you*	gehst	brauchst	kaufst	kommst	(*you go*; *you need*; *you buy*; *you come*)
er *he*	geht	braucht	kauft	kommt	(*he goes*; *he needs*; *he buys*; *he comes*)
sie *she*	geht	braucht	kauft	kommt	(*she goes*; *she needs*; *she buys*; *she comes*)
es *it*	geht	braucht	kauft	kommt	(*it goes*; *it needs*; *it buys*; *it comes*)
wir *we*	gehen	brauchen	kaufen	kommen	(*we go*; *we need*; *we buy*; *we come*)
ihr *you*	geht	braucht	kauft	kommt	(*you go*; *you need*; *you buy*; *you come*)
Sie *you*	gehen	brauchen	kaufen	kommen	(*you go*; *you need*; *you buy*; *you come*)
sie *they*	gehen	brauchen	kaufen	kommen	(*they go*; *they need*; *they buy*; *they come*)

To say good-bye to someone you are speaking with in person, say **Auf Wiedersehen.** (*Until I see you again.*) But on the phone, say **Auf Wiederhören.** (*Until I hear from you again.*)

TRACK 18

Listen to the following questions and answers on your CD. After you hear a phrase or sentence on a track, always press "pause" and repeat what you hear.

Geht Dirk ins Einkaufszentrum?	*Is Dirk going to the mall?*
Ja, er geht ins Einkaufszentrum.	*Yes, he is going to the mall.*
Brauchst du eine Jacke?	*Do you need a jacket?*
Ja, ich brauche eine Jacke.	*Yes, I need a jacket.*
Kaufst du ein Glas?	*Are you buying a glass?*
Nein, ich kaufe ein Brot.	*No, I am buying a loaf of bread.*
Kommt Renate auch mit?	*Is Renate also coming along?*
Ja, Renate kommt auch mit.	*Yes, Renate is also coming along.*
Geht ihr nach Hause?	*Are you going home?*
Ja, wir gehen nach Hause.	*Yes, we are going home.*
Brauchen Sie eine Jacke, Herr Braun?	*Do you need a jacket, Mr. Braun?*
Nein, ich brauche ein Hemd.	*No, I need a shirt.*
Kaufen sie eine Lampe?	*Are they buying a lamp?*
Nein, sie kaufen einen Stuhl.	*No, they are buying a chair.*
Kommt Ingrid mit?	*Is Ingrid coming along?*
Nein, sie kommt nicht mit.	*No, she is not coming along.*

Oral Practice 4-1

TRACK 19

Listen to your CD to hear each new noun pronounced. Press "pause" and repeat what you hear; then ask whether *Dirk is buying* that item. Listen to your CD to hear the correct answer, making sure to repeat what you hear. For example:

> die Jacke *jacket*
> *You say:* Kauft Dirk die Jacke?

das Hemd *shirt*

das Kleid *dress*

die Schuhe *shoes*

der Hut *hat*

die Hose *pants*

die Socken *socks*

die Handschuhe *gloves*

der Rock *skirt*

GRAMMAR DEMYSTIFIED

Definite and Indefinite Articles

The definite articles **der**, **die**, and **das** mean *the*. The German indefinite articles (*a*, *an* in English) are **ein** for masculine and neuter nouns and **eine** for feminine nouns: **ein Mann** (*a man*), **ein Haus** (*a house*), **eine Lampe** (*a lamp*). If a noun is plural, the indefinite article is not used: **Schuhe** (*shoes*), **Socken** (*socks*).

TRACK 20

Now listen to the questions on your CD that ask *what you are buying*. After each question press "pause" to repeat what you hear, and then, using the noun in parentheses as your cue, answer the question appropriately. Then listen to the correct answer and repeat it. For example:

Was kaufen Sie? (*jacket*)	*What are you buying?*
You say: Ich kaufe eine Jacke.	*I am buying a jacket.*

Was kaufen Sie? (*shirt*)

Was kaufen Sie? (*lamp*)

Was kaufen Sie? (*shoes*)

Was kaufen Sie? (*dress*)

Was kaufen Sie? (*socks*)

Was kaufen Sie? (*bread*)

Was kaufen Sie? (*blouse*)

Was kaufen Sie? (*skirt*)

Was kaufen Sie? (*pants*)

Was kaufen Sie? (*gloves*)

Oral Practice 4-2

Read each question out loud. Then, using the word provided in parentheses as your cue, answer the question appropriately. Cover the correct answers shown on the right, listen to them on the CD, and repeat what you hear. Use them to compare with your own answers. For example:

Was kaufst du? (*shirt*)
You say: Ich kaufe ein Hemd.

Was kauft Renate? (*blouse*)	Renate kauft eine Bluse.
Was kaufen Erik und Sabine? (*bread*)	Erik und Sabine kaufen ein Brot.
Was kauft er? (*hat*)	Er kauft einen Hut.
Was kaufen Sie? (*jacket*)	Ich kaufe eine Jacke.
Was kauft ihr? (*socks*)	Wir kaufen Socken.
Was braucht Dirk? (*gloves*)	Dirk braucht Handschuhe.
Was braucht ihr? (*shoes*)	Wir brauchen Schuhe.
Was braucht sie? (*dress*)	Sie braucht ein Kleid.
Was brauchen wir? (*lamp*)	Ihr braucht eine Lampe.
Was brauchen Sie? (*skirt*)	Ich brauche einen Rock.

Asking Questions with *Haben*

Look at the following examples of asking a question using the verb **haben**. Practice asking and answering each question out loud.

Hast du ein Glas?	*Do you have a glass?*
Ja, ich habe ein Glas.	*Yes, I have a glass.*
Hat Dirk ein Hemd?	*Does Dirk have a shirt?*
Nein, er hat einen Hut.	*No, he has a hat.*
Hat Renate eine Bluse?	*Does Renate have a blouse?*
Ja, sie hat eine Bluse.	*Yes, she has a blouse.*

GRAMMAR DEMYSTIFIED

The Verbs *Haben* and *Sein*

Two very important verbs in German are **haben** (*to have*) and **sein** (*to be*). They have a very high-frequency use in German, and their conjugations in the present tense break the pattern for verbs that was illustrated earlier. Let's look at these two verbs with all the pronouns.

Pronoun	**sein**	**haben**	(*to be*; *to have*)
ich *I*	bin	habe	(*I am*; *I have*)
du *you*	bist	hast	(*you are*; *you have*)
er *he*	ist	hat	(*he is*; *he has*)
sie *she*	ist	hat	(*she is*; *she has*)
es *it*	ist	hat	(*it is*; *it has*)
wir *we*	sind	haben	(*we are*; *we have*)
ihr *you*	seid	habt	(*you are*; *you have*)
Sie *you*	sind	haben	(*you are*; *you have*)
sie *they*	sind	haben	(*they are*; *they have*)

Haben Sie eine Schwester?	*Do you have a sister?*
Nein, ich habe einen Bruder.	*No, I have a brother.*
Habt ihr Handschuhe?	*Do you have gloves?*
Ja, wir haben Handschuhe.	*Yes, we have gloves.*
Haben sie ein Brot?	*Do they have a loaf of bread?*
Nein, sie haben eine Wurst.	*No, they have a sausage.*
Haben Sie einen Rock?	*Do you have a skirt?*
Ja, ich habe einen Rock.	*Yes, I have a skirt.*

VOCABULARY DEMYSTIFIED

Zu Hause/Nach Hause

You have already learned that **nach Hause** is the expression used to say that someone is *going home*. The expression **zu Hause** is similar but means that someone is *at home*. To ask where someone is, use the interrogative word **wo** (*where*). Common responses to **wo** are: **hier** and **da** or **dort** (*here* and *there*).

Asking Questions with *Sein*

The verb **sein** is used in many questions that ask where someone or something is. Recite each of the following questions and answers out loud to practice using the verb **sein**.

Wo ist der Mann?	*Where is the man?*
Der Mann ist zu Hause.	*The man is at home.*

Wo ist Frau Schneider?	*Where is Ms. Schneider?*
Frau Schneider ist in Berlin.	*Ms. Schneider is in Berlin.*
Wo bist du?	*Where are you?*
Ich bin hier.	*I am here.*
Wo sind Dirk und Renate?	*Where are Dirk and Renate?*
Dirk und Renate sind da.	*Dirk and Renate are there.*
Wo seid ihr?	*Where are you?*
Wir sind zu Hause.	*We are at home.*
Wo sind sie?	*Where are they?*
Sie sind in Deutschland.	*They are in Germany.*
Wo sind Sie?	*Where are you?*
Ich bin in Österreich.	*I am in Austria.*

Oral Practice 4-3

 **TRACK 22**

Using the German verbs and English nouns provided as your cues, ask *what Frau Schneider does*. Then listen to your CD for the correct question. Press "pause" and repeat what you hear. Then respond to the question. Listen to the correct response on the CD, and again repeat what you hear. For example:

kaufen, *shirt*
You say: Was kauft Frau Schneider? Frau Schneider kauft ein Hemd.

kaufen, *bread*

haben, *blouse*

brauchen, *shoes*

kaufen, *chair*

haben, *gloves*

brauchen, *dress*

kaufen, *lamp*

haben, *skirt*

Asking Where Someone Is Traveling Using *Wo* and *Wohin*

When traveling to a city or country, use the verb **reisen** and the preposition **nach** (**ich reise nach**, **du reist nach**, **er reist nach**, [*I travel to*, *you travel to*, *he travels to*] and so on): **Ich reise nach Deutschland.** (*I travel to Germany.*) To ask *where* someone is traveling, use the interrogative word **wohin** (*where to*): **Wohin reisen Sie?** (*Where are you traveling* [*to*]*?*) Use **wo** to ask about locations.

wo = location	**wohin** = motion to a place
Wo ist Karl? *Where is Karl?*	Wohin reisen Sie? *Where are you traveling?*
Wo sind wir? *Where are we?*	Wohin geht Tina? *Where is Tina going?*

Look at the following questions and answers, and note the different uses of **wo** and **wohin**:

Wo ist Astrid?	*Where is Astrid?*
Astrid ist zu Hause.	*Astrid is at home.*
Wo ist der Stadtpark?	*Where is the city park?*
Der Stadtpark ist weit von hier.	*The city park is far from here.*
Wohin reist du?	*Where are you traveling?*
Ich reise nach Bonn.	*I am traveling to Bonn.*

Wohin reist Dirk?	*Where is Dirk traveling?*
Dirk reist nach Paris.	*Dirk is traveling to Paris.*

Oral Practice 4-4

TRACK 23

Listen to the questions on your CD that ask *where someone is traveling.* After each question, press "pause" and repeat the question. Then, using the name of the country or city provided in parentheses, answer the question appropriately. After you hear a phrase or sentence on a track, always press "pause" and repeat what you hear. For example:

Wohin reisen Sie? (Deutschland *Germany*)
You say: Ich reise nach Deutschland.

Wohin reist du? (Amerika *America*)

Wohin reist Erik? (Österreich *Austria*)

Wohin reist Frau Keller? (Polen *Poland*)

Wohin reisen sie? (Frankreich *France*)

Wohin reist ihr? (England *England*)

Wohin reisen Karl und Otto? (Italien *Italy*)

Wohin reisen wir? (Paris *Paris*)

Wohin reise ich? (München *Munich*)

Wohin reist sie? (Rom *Rome*)

Wohin reist Professor Benz? (Zürich *Zurich*)

Written Practice 4-1

Complete each question by filling in the interrogative word **wo** or **wohin** appropriately.

1. _______________ wohnen Sie, Herr Keller?
2. _______________ geht Doktor Schmidt?

3. ______________ ist die Schule?
4. ______________ reist der Tourist?
5. ______________ sind Herr Braun und Frau Bauer?

GRAMMAR DEMYSTIFIED

Present Tense Endings with *Du*

The typical present tense ending used with verbs that follow **du** is **-st**. But if the stem of the verb ends with a sibilant sound (**-s**, **-ss**, **-ß**), only the letter **-t** is added to the stem.

reisen	du reist
heißen	du heißt

Written Practice 4-2

The following lines of dialogue are out of sequence. Place a number, from 1 to 9, in each blank to show the appropriate order for the lines.

______ Ist dein Bruder zu Hause?

______ Wie geht's, Felix?

______ Tschüs, Sabine.

______ Ganz gut. Sabine, hast du heute nachmittag Zeit?

______ Ich möchte einkaufen gehen. Ich brauche ein Hemd.

______ Nein, er ist in Frankreich.

______ Auf Wiederhören, Felix!

______ Nein, ich muss heute nachmittag lernen.

______ Wie schön!

VOCABULARY DEMYSTIFIED

Greetings in a Shop

When you enter a shop or store in Germany, it is common to say hello to the clerk: **Guten Tag.** And upon leaving, you will probably hear **Auf Wiedersehen**, which you should also offer as a courtesy.

QUIZ

TRACK 24

Responding to questions. Listen to your CD to hear each question. Press "pause" to repeat the question out loud and select your answer—a, b, or c. Then listen to the correct answer on the CD, making sure to repeat what you hear.

1. (a) Nein, sie ist in Deutschland.
   (b) Nein, er hat morgen eine Prüfung.
   (c) Nein, mein Bruder ist hier.

2. (a) Heute nachmittag.
   (b) Wie schön!
   (c) Ein Kleid.

3. (a) Ein Hemd.
   (b) Auf Wiederhören!
   (c) Frankreich.

4. (a) Nicht weit von hier.
   (b) Nach Deutschland.
   (c) Zum Einkaufszentrum.

5. (a) Er reist nach Italien.
   (b) Ich reise nach Zürich.
   (c) Sie reisen nach Hause.

Using the cue words provided, say that the person (or persons) has the item. Listen to the correct answer on the CD, making sure to repeat what you hear. For example:

der Mann, ein Hemd
You say: Der Mann hat ein Hemd.

6. Renate, eine Bluse
7. Sie, einen Hut
8. Erik und Felix, ein Problem
9. ich, eine Lampe
10. ihr, Socken und Schuhe

CHAPTER 5

Celebrating Birthdays

In this chapter you will learn:

Talking About der Geburtstag *(the Birthday)*

Zahlen *Numbers*

Ordinal Numbers

Months of the Year

Describing Age

Talking About *der Geburtstag* (the Birthday)

 TRACK 25

Listen to the following dialogue on your CD. After you hear a phrase or sentence on a track, always press "pause" and repeat what you hear.

WERNER: Sag mal, wann hast du Geburtstag? *Hey, when is your birthday?*

GABI: Am Zehnten dieses Monats. *On the tenth of this month.*

WERNER: Wie alt wirst du? Achtzehn oder neunzehn? — *How old will you be? Eighteen or nineteen?*

GABI: Ich kann es nicht glauben. Ich werde neunzehn. — *I cannot believe it. I will be nineteen.*

WERNER: Gabi, das ist gar nicht alt. — *Gabi, that is not at all old.*

GABI: Ich weiß. Aber es ist auch nicht jung. — *I know. But it is not young either.*

WERNER: Wo feierst du deinen Geburtstag? — *Where will you celebrate your birthday?*

GABI: Wir machen ein kleines Fest im Wohnzimmer. — *We will have a little party in the living room.*

WERNER: Was wünschst du dir zum Geburtstag? — *What do you want for your birthday?*

GABI: Ich hätte gern einen neuen CD-Spieler. — *I would like a new CD player.*

WERNER: Toll! Ich bringe dir eine CD. — *Great! I will bring you a CD.*

Dialogue Review

Answer the following questions about the dialogue Talking About **der Geburtstag** out loud. Cover the correct answers shown on the right. Use them to compare with your own answers.

1. Wann hat Gabi Geburtstag? *When is Gabi's birthday?* — Sie hat am Zehnten dieses Monats Geburtstag.

2. Wie alt wird Gabi? *How old is Gabi going to be?* — Sie wird neunzehn.

3. Was hätte sie gern? *What would she like to have?* — Sie hätte gern einen neuen CD-Spieler.

ZAHLEN NUMBERS

TRACK 26

Listen to your CD to hear the following pairs of numbers pronounced. After every two numbers, press "pause" and repeat what you heard.

eins, zwei (1, 2)

drei, vier (3, 4)

fünf, sechs (5, 6)

sieben, acht (7, 8)

neun, zehn (9, 10)

elf, zwölf (11, 12)

dreizehn, vierzehn (13, 14)

fünfzehn, sechzehn (15, 16)

siebzehn, achtzehn (17, 18)

neunzehn, zwanzig (19, 20)

dreißig, vierzig (30, 40)

fünfzig, sechzig (50, 60)

siebzig, achtzig (70, 80)

neunzig, hundert (90, 100)

tausend, zweitausend (1,000; 2,000)

The numbers from 21 to 99 in German have a slightly different form from their English counterparts. It's similar to the phrase from the children's nursery rhyme: "four and twenty blackbirds baked in a pie." In German, you would say *four and twenty* rather than *twenty-four*: **vierundzwanzig**. This occurs with all numbers from 21 to 99. Look at the following examples and practice saying them out loud:

einundzwanzig	21	achtundfünfzig	58
zweiundzwanzig	22	neunundsechzig	69
dreiunddreißig	33	hunderteinundsechzig	161
vierunddreißig	34	hundertzweiundsiebzig	172
fünfundvierzig	45	hundertdreiundneunzig	193
sechsundvierzig	46	zweihunderteins	201
siebenundfünfzig	57	dreihundertvierundzwanzig	324

Numbers are commonly used in arithmetic expressions. In an addition statement, combine two numbers with **plus** or **und**: **Zwei plus drei ist fünf. Vier und fünf ist neun.** In subtraction, subtract one number from another by using the words **minus** or **weniger**: **Vierzehn minus zwei ist zwölf. Acht weniger sieben ist eins.** Questions for addition and subtraction begin with the words **wie viel** (*how much*).

Wie viel ist drei plus drei?

Drei plus drei ist sechs.

Wie viel ist neun minus zwei? (*How much is nine minus two?*)

Neun minus zwei ist sieben. (*Nine minus two is seven.*)

Written Practice 5-1

Write each equation as a question, and then write out its appropriate answer in a complete sentence. For example:

2 + 1 *Wie viel ist zwei plus eins? Zwei plus eins ist drei.*

1. 4 + 5 ______________________________
2. 7 − 3 ______________________________
3. 10 + 6 ______________________________
4. 20 − 9 ______________________________
5. 40 + 30 ______________________________
6. 90 − 50 ______________________________
7. 33 + 2 ______________________________
8. 80 − 41 ______________________________
9. 11 + 12 ______________________________
10. 100 − 99 ______________________________

ORDINAL NUMBERS

In the dialogue, Gabi said that her birthday was on the tenth of the month: **am Zehnten des Monats**. To change a cardinal number to an ordinal number, say **am ... -ten** with numbers under twenty and **am ... -sten** with numbers twenty and larger.

am Zweiten *on the tenth*

am Elften *on the eleventh*

am Zwanzigsten *on the twentieth*

am Einunddreißigsten *on the thirty-first*

Three ordinal numbers have a slightly irregular form:

am Ersten *on the first*

am Dritten *on the third*

am Siebten *on the seventh*

Look at the following questions and answers, and practice saying each one out loud:

Wann hast du Geburtstag? *When is your birthday?*

Am Ersten dieses Monats. *On the first of this month.*

Wann haben Sie Geburtstag? *When is your birthday?*

Am Vierten dieses Monats. *On the fourth of this month.*

Wann hat Erik Geburtstag? *When is Erik's birthday?*

Am Zwölften dieses Monats. *On the twelfth of this month.*

Wann hat Gabi Geburtstag? *When is Gabi's birthday?*

Am Neunzehnten dieses Monats. *On the nineteenth of this month.*

Wann ist die Party?	*When is the party?*
Am Einundzwanzigsten dieses Monats.	*On the twenty-first of this month.*
Wann ist das Fest?	*When is the party?*
Am Sechsundzwanzigsten dieses Monats.	*On the twenty-sixth of this month.*
Wann ist die Prüfung?	*When is the test?*
Am Dreißigsten dieses Monats.	*On the thirtieth of this month.*

Oral Practice 5-1

 TRACK 27

Using the noun and number cues provided, say on what day of the month each event is taking place. Listen to the correct answers on your CD. Press "pause" and repeat what you hear. For example:

die Party, 11
You say: Die Party ist am Elften dieses Monats.

das Fest, 3

Gabis Geburtstag, 15

die Party, 22

die Prüfung, 7

Werners Geburtstag, 31

MONTHS OF THE YEAR

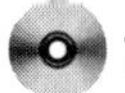 TRACK 28

Listen to your CD to hear dates and months in some useful sentences. Press "pause" after each sentence and repeat what you hear.

Heute ist der erste Januar.	*Today is the first of January.*
Heute ist der zweite Februar.	*Today is the second of February.*
Heute ist der dritte März.	*Today is the third of March.*
Heute ist der zehnte April.	*Today is the tenth of April.*
Heute ist der zwölfte Mai.	*Today is the twelfth of May.*
Heute ist der sechzehnte Juni.	*Today is the sixteenth of June.*
Morgen ist der neunzehnte Juli.	*Tomorrow is the nineteenth of July.*
Morgen ist der zwanzigste August.	*Tomorrow is the twentieth of August.*
Morgen ist der zweiundzwanzigste September.	*Tomorrow is the twenty-second of September.*
Morgen ist der achtundzwanzigste Oktober.	*Tomorrow is the twenty-eighth of October.*
Morgen ist der dreißigste November.	*Tomorrow is the thirtieth of November.*
Morgen ist der einunddreißigste Dezember.	*Tomorrow is the thirty-first of December.*
Ich bin am zweiten Juni geboren.	*I was born on the second of June.*
Er ist am neunten Januar geboren.	*He was born on the ninth of January.*
Sie ist am siebzehnten März geboren.	*She was born on the seventeenth of March.*

GRAMMAR DEMYSTIFIED

Dates

Careful! When a German date is given in numbers, the *day* precedes the *month*, which is the opposite of how it appears in English.

6/5	*May 6*
2/9	*September 2*

Practice saying the following German words for the members of a family:

dein Vater *your father*	mein Vater *my father*
deine Mutter *your mother*	meine Mutter *my mother*
dein Großvater *your grandfather*	mein Großvater *my grandfather*
deine Großmutter *your grandmother*	meine Großmutter *my grandmother*
dein Sohn *your son*	mein Sohn *my son*
deine Tochter *your daughter*	meine Tochter *my daughter*
deine Kinder *your children*	meine Kinder *my children*
deine Eltern *your parents*	meine Eltern *my parents*

Oral Practice 5-2

Use the nouns provided as your cues to ask when each person was born. Listen to your CD to hear the correct question. Press "pause" to repeat what you hear, and then, using the dates in parentheses, answer each question appropriately. Then listen to the correct answer, making sure to repeat what you hear. For example:

son (5/11)
You say: Wann ist dein Sohn geboren? Mein Sohn ist am fünften November geboren.

father (1/1)

mother (16/9)

grandfather (4/7)

grandmother (24/12)

female teacher (28/2)

daughter (31/10)

parents (5/3)

children (23/8)

DESCRIBING AGE

When describing the age of a person you can use **jung** (*young*) or **alt** (*old*). Look at the following questions and answers, and practice them out loud:

Ist dein Vater jung oder alt?	*Is your father young or old?*
Mein Vater ist jung.	*My father is young.*
Ist dein Bruder jung oder alt?	*Is your brother young or old?*
Mein Bruder ist alt.	*My brother is old.*
Ist deine Schwester jung oder alt?	*Is your sister young or old?*
Meine Schwester ist jung.	*My sister is young.*
Ist deine Großmutter jung oder alt?	*Is your grandmother young or old?*
Meine Großmutter ist alt.	*My grandmother is old.*

We can also use the word **alt** to describe the age of something:

Ist dein Wagen alt oder neu?	*Is your car old or new?*
Mein Wagen ist neu.	*My car is new.*
Ist dein Haus alt oder neu?	*Is your house old or new?*
Mein Haus ist alt.	*My house is old.*
Ist deine CD alt oder neu?	*Is your CD old or new?*
Meine CD ist neu.	*My CD is new.*
Ist deine Hose alt oder neu?	*Are your pants old or new?*
Meine Hose ist alt.	*My pants are old.*

Oral Practice 5-3

 TRACK 30

Listen to each question on your CD. Press "pause" and repeat the question. Answer the question with the appropriate word that is the opposite of old: **jung** or **neu**. Then listen to the correct answer, making sure to repeat what you hear. For example:

> Ist dein Haus alt?
> *You say*: Nein, mein Haus ist neu.

Ist dein Buch alt?

Ist dein Wagen alt?

Ist deine Mutter alt?

Ist deine Lehrerin alt?

Ist deine Bluse alt?

Ist dein Professor alt?

Sind deine Handschuhe alt?

Sind deine Eltern alt?

Sind deine Kinder alt?

Sind Werner und Gabi alt?

CULTURE DEMYSTIFIED

Birthday Parties

If you're invited to a **Geburtstagsfeier** (*birthday party*), be sure to take along a little token as a **Geburtstagsgeschenk** (*birthday present*). You can expect to feast on a **Geburtstagstorte** (*birthday cake*). Be sure to wish the **Geburtstagskind** (*birthday boy* or *girl*) a "Happy Birthday": **Herzliche Glückwünsche zum Geburtstag!**

Written Practice 5-2

The following lines of dialogue are out of sequence. Place a number, from 1 to 8, in each blank to show the appropriate order for the lines.

_____ Sabine ist so jung.

_____ Ist sie zwanzig oder einundzwanzig?

_____ Am Dritten dieses Monats.

_____ Herr Keller ist achtzig.

_____ Ich weiß nicht. Ich glaube zwanzig.

_____ Ja, aber Herr Keller ist alt.

_____ Wann hat Sabine Keller Geburtstag?

_____ Wie alt ist er?

PHRASES FOR SURVIVAL

Age

Add these useful phrases to your language arsenal to help you get by in the German-speaking world:

Wie alt sind Sie?	*How old are you?*
Ich bin dreiunddreißig Jahre alt.	*I am thirty-three years old.*
Thomas is ungefähr zwanzig.	*Thomas is approximately twenty.*
Tina ist Mitte vierzig.	*Tina is in her mid-forties.*
Mein Sohn ist gerade zehn geworden.	*My son just turned ten.*
Sabine ist noch keine achtzehn Jahre alt.	*Sabine is not even eighteen yet.*
Erik ist noch ein Teenager.	*Erik is still a teenager.*

QUIZ

TRACK 31

Responding to questions. Listen to your CD to hear each question. Press "pause" to repeat the question out loud and select your answer—a, b, or c. Then listen to the correct answer on the CD, making sure to repeat what you hear.

1. (a) Morgen ist der Zehnte.
   (b) Am Elften dieses Monats.
   (c) Frau Bauer ist vierzig.

2. (a) Nein, meine Bluse ist neu.
   (b) Ja, sie ist jung.
   (c) Nein, sie ist braun.

3. (a) Hundertdrei.
   (b) Dreiundfünfzig.
   (c) Dreiundsiebzig.

4. (a) Am neunzehnten Februar.
   (b) Heute ist der Dritte.
   (c) Morgen ist der Zweite.

5. (a) Er ist alt.
   (b) Nein, er ist nicht jung.
   (c) Er ist am Achten dieses Monats geboren.

Using the cues provided, say that the person was born on the date indicated. Listen to the correct answer on the CD, making sure to repeat what you hear. For example:

der Mann, 9/10
You say: Der Mann ist am Neunten Oktober geboren.

6. die Frau, 11/2
7. mein Sohn, 23/6
8. dein Vater, 3/11

Using the nouns provided as your cues, say *that the person is not old. He or she is young*. Listen to the correct answer on the CD, making sure to repeat what you hear. For example:

grandfather
You say: Mein Großvater ist nicht alt. Er ist jung.

9. *grandmother*
10. *brother*

PART ONE TEST

TRACK 32

Responding to questions. Listen to your CD to hear each question. Press "pause" to repeat the question out loud and select your answer—a, b, or c. Then listen to the correct answer on the CD, making sure to repeat what you hear.

1. (a) Der Lehrer.
   (b) Nach Hause.
   (c) Gut, danke.

2. (a) Erik.
   (b) Herr Schneider.
   (c) Sabine.

3. (a) Das ist Frau Keller.
   (b) Das ist der Mann.
   (c) Das ist die Jacke.

4. (a) Das ist meine Mutter.
   (b) Das ist die Lampe.
   (c) Das ist der Hut.

5. (a) Nein, zum Bahnhof.
   (b) Guten Morgen.
   (c) Nein, in Berlin.

6. (a) Nein, es geht Sabine gut.
   (b) Ja, sie ist Lehrerin.
   (c) Gut, danke.

7. (a) Ja, sie geht zum Restaurant.
   (b) Nein, sie geht zur Party.
   (c) Ja, sie ist in Deutschland.

8. (a) Eine Bluse.
   (b) Wie schön!
   (c) Das Kind.

9. (a) Nicht weit von hier.
   (b) Auf Wiederhören!
   (c) Einen Hut.

10. (a) In Frankreich.
    (b) Nach Deutschland.
    (c) Zum Einkaufszentrum.

11. (a) Er reist nach Italien.
    (b) Ich reise nach Zürich.
    (c) Sie reist nach Österreich.

12. (a) Morgen ist der Zehnte.
    (b) Am Elften dieses Monats.
    (c) Sie ist vierzig.

13. (a) Nein, es ist alt.
    (b) Ja, sie ist jung.
    (c) Nein, er ist braun.

14. (a) Hundertdrei.
    (b) Dreiundfünfzig.
    (c) Achtundsechzig.

15. (a) Am dritten Juni.
    (b) Heute ist der Elfte.
    (c) Morgen ist der Zweite.

Using each word or phrase provided as your cue, ask either *who that is* or *what that is*. Then answer the question appropriately. Listen to the correct answers on your CD, making sure to repeat what you hear. For example:

tourist
You say: Wer ist das? Das ist der Tourist.

16. *female teacher*
17. *shirt*
18. *lamp*

Say the following English phrases in German out loud. Listen to the correct answers on your CD.

19. *Good morning.*
20. *Good afternoon.*
21. *Good-bye.*

Decide whether the following questions begin with **wo** or **wohin** appropriately. Listen to the correct answers on your CD, making sure to repeat what you hear.

22. Wo *or* Wohin geht Herr Keller?
23. Wo *or* Wohin ist deine Tochter?

Using the cues provided, say that the person has the item. Then listen to the correct answer on the CD, making sure to repeat what you hear. For example:

der Mann, ein Hemd
You say: Der Mann hat ein Hemd.

24. Frau Schäfer, eine Bluse
25. Ich, ein Hemd

PART TWO

OUT AND ABOUT

CHAPTER 6

Getting Sick

In this chapter you will learn:

Das Kranksein *Getting Sick*

Expressing "Like" Using Haben ... gern

Future Tense

Das Kranksein Getting Sick

 TRACK 33

Listen to the following dialogue on your CD. After you hear a phrase or sentence on a track, always press "pause" and repeat what you hear.

JÜRGEN: Was ist mit Erik los? Ist er müde?	*What is the matter with Erik? Is he tired?*
GABRIELE: Er fühlt sich nicht wohl. Er ist krank.	*He does not feel well. He is sick.*

JÜRGEN: Er hustet ja fürchterlich.	*And he has a terrible cough.*
GABRIELE: Ich glaube, er hat sich wieder erkältet.	*I think he has caught a cold again.*
JÜRGEN: Hat er Fieber?	*Does he have a fever?*
GABRIELE: Leider. Und der Hals tut ihm weh.	*Unfortunately. And he has a sore throat.*
JÜRGEN: Soll er sich nicht hinlegen?	*Shouldn't he lie down?*
GABRIELE: Nein, ich will ihn zum Arzt bringen.	*No, I want to take him to the doctor.*
JÜRGEN: Gute Idee. Ich werde Doktor Benz anrufen.	*Good idea. I will call Dr. Benz.*

Dialogue Review

Answer the following questions about the dialogue **Das Kranksein** out loud. Cover the correct answers shown on the right. Use them to compare with your own answers.

1. Wer ist krank? — Erik ist krank.
   Who is sick?
2. Was tut Erik weh? — Der Hals tut Erik weh.
   Where does Erik hurt?
3. Was will Gabriele tun? — Sie will Erik zum Arzt bringen.
   What does Gabriele want to do?

When asking *what the matter is with someone*, this useful phrase comes in handy: **Was ist mit ... los?** Just insert a name (or pronoun) into the phrase. For example:

Was ist mit Martin los?	*What is the matter with Martin?*
Was ist mit Gabriele los?	*What is the matter with Gabriele?*

Was ist mit Doktor Keller los? *What is the matter with Dr. Keller?*

Was ist mit Frau Schneider los? *What is the matter with Ms. Schneider?*

Expressing "Like" Using *Haben ... gern*

You already know the verb **haben** (*to have*). It is used together with the word **gern** to mean *to like*. For example:

Ich habe Jürgen gern. *I like Jürgen.*

Sie hat ihn gern. *She likes him.*

Hast du uns gern? *Do you like us?*

GRAMMAR DEMYSTIFIED

Direct Objects

When an action is *performed on* a person or thing, that person or thing is called a *direct object*. In German, direct objects are said to be in the accusative case. And just as English pronouns change form when they are direct objects, German pronouns change from their nominative case form to their accusative case form when they are direct objects. Let's compare the nominative case pronouns (the subject of a sentence) with the accusative case pronouns:

Nominative Case	**Accusative Case**
Ich *I*	mich *me*
du *you*	dich *you*
er *he*	ihn *him*
sie *she*	sie *her*
es *it*	es *it*
wir *we*	uns *us*
ihr *you*	euch *you*
Sie *you*	Sie *you*
sie *they*	sie *them*
wer *whom*	wen *whom*
was *what*	was *what*

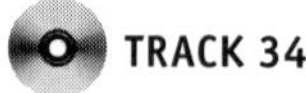 **TRACK 34**

On your CD listen to the following sentences that use **haben ... gern**. Press "pause" after each sentence and repeat what you hear.

Haben Sie Frau Keller gern?	*Do you like Ms. Keller?*
Ja, ich habe sie gern.	*Yes, I like her.*
Haben Sie Gabriele gern?	*Do you like Gabriele?*
Ja, ich habe sie gern.	*Yes, I like her.*
Hast du Doktor Benz gern?	*Do you like Dr. Benz?*
Ja, ich habe ihn gern.	*Yes, I like him.*
Hast du Erik und Sabine gern?	*Do you like Erik and Sabine?*
Ja, ich habe sie gern.	*Yes, I like them.*
Ich glaube, Martin hat mich gern.	*I think Martin likes me.*
Ich glaube, sie haben dich gern.	*I think they like you.*
Der Arzt hat uns gern.	*The doctor likes us.*
Der Lehrer hat euch gern.	*The teacher likes you.*

Oral Practice 6-1

 **TRACK 35**

Say each question out loud. Then respond using the appropriate accusative pronoun. Listen to the correct answers on the CD and repeat what you hear. For example:

Hast du Werner gern?
You say: Ja, ich habe ihn gern.

Hast du Gabriele gern?

Hat Erik Sabine und Tanja gern?

Hat Martin Jürgen und mich gern?

Haben Sie Thomas gern?

Hat Herr Kohl Frau Keller gern?

Haben die Kinder mich gern?

Hat der Arzt dich gern?

Haben wir Erik gern?

GRAMMAR DEMYSTIFIED

Some Useful New Verbs

The following four verbs, **besuchen** (*to visit*), **finden** (*to find*), **hören** (*to hear*), and **sehen** (*to see*), will come in handy in many situations. Notice that **finden** and **sehen** have a slight irregularity to remember.

Pronoun	**besuchen**	**finden**	**hören**	**sehen**
ich	besuche	finde	höre	sehe
du	besuchst	find**est**	hörst	**sie**hst
er, sie, es	besucht	find**et**	hört	**sie**ht
wir	besuchen	finden	hören	sehen
ihr	besucht	find**et**	hört	seht
Sie	besuchen	finden	hören	sehen
sie	besuchen	finden	hören	sehen

Oral Practice 6-2

TRACK 36

Listen to each of the following nouns pronounced on your CD. Press “pause” to repeat each one as you hear it. Then ask whether *they see* that object. Listen to the correct answers on the CD and repeat what you hear. For example:

der Park *park*
You say: Sehen sie den Park?

das Museum *museum*

das Kino *movie theater*

die Brücke *bridge*

der Flughafen *airport*

das Flugzeug *airplane*

der Bahnhof *train station*

der Zug *train*

die Bushaltestelle *bus stop*

der Bus *bus*

der Wagen *car*

Written Practice 6-1

Using the nouns provided as your cues, write questions asking *where someone* or *something is.* Then say *Jürgen sees* that person or thing. For example:

school
You write: Wo ist die Schule? Jürgen sieht die Schule.

1. *bus* ______
2. *jacket* ______
3. *train station* ______
4. *car* ______
5. *bridge* ______
6. *gloves* ______
7. *airport* ______
8. *museum* ______
9. *movie theater* ______
10. *bus stop* ______

GRAMMAR DEMYSTIFIED

Masculine Direct Objects

When a masculine noun is used as a direct object, the articles **der** and **ein** change to their accusative case forms: **den** and **einen**. Feminine, neuter, and plural nouns make no changes. For example:

Nominative Case	**Accusative Case**
Wo ist der Mann? *Where is the man?*	Siehst du **den** Mann? *Do you see the man?*
Wo ist der Bus? *Where is the bus?*	Siehst du **den** Bus? *Do you see the bus?*
Wo ist der Arzt? *Where is the doctor?*	Siehst du **den** Arzt? *Do you see the doctor?*
Wo ist die Frau? *Where is the woman?*	Siehst du die Frau? *Do you see the woman?*
Wo ist das Kind? *Where is the child?*	Siehst du das Kind? *Do you see the child?*
Wo sind die Kinder? *Where are the children?*	Siehst du die Kinder? *Do you see the children?*

Oral Practice 6-3

TRACK 37

Recite out loud the following sentences that contain direct objects. Say the question; then answer it appropriately with **ja**. Cover the correct answers shown on the right, listen to them on the CD, and repeat what you hear. For example:

Siehst du den Bus?
You say: Ja, ich sehe den Bus.

Siehst du das Museum?	Ja, ich sehe das Museum.
Kaufst du einen Hut?	Ja, ich kaufe einen Hut.
Hörst du den Professor?	Ja, ich höre den Professor.
Brauchst du einen Stuhl?	Ja, ich brauche einen Stuhl.
Findest du eine Jacke?	Ja, ich finde eine Jacke.
Besuchst du deine Eltern?	Ja, ich besuche meine Eltern.

Bringst du eine CD?	Ja, ich bringe eine CD.
Feierst du deinen Geburtstag?	Ja, ich feiere meinen Geburtstag.

Now answer the questions with **nein**, and change the direct object in each question to the one in parentheses. For example:

Siehst du den Mann? (die Frau)
You say: Nein, ich sehe die Frau.

Hast du eine Lampe? (ein Hut)	Nein, ich habe einen Hut.
Siehst du den Zug? (der Bus)	Nein, ich sehe den Bus.
Hörst du die Lehrerin? (der Professor)	Nein, ich höre den Professor.
Besuchst du deine Großmutter? (dein Großvater)	Nein, ich besuche meinen Großvater.
Findest du ein Glas? (eine Lampe)	Nein, ich finde eine Lampe.
Hast du sie gern? (er)	Nein, ich habe ihn gern.
Brauchst du ein Brot? (ein Kuchen)	Nein, ich brauche einen Kuchen.

Written Practice 6-2

Fill in each blank with the appropriate form of the verb in parentheses.

1. Er _______________ den Arzt. (sehen)
2. _______________ du eine Bushaltestelle? (sehen)
3. Ich _______________ Frau Schneider. (sehen)
4. Was _______________ Gabriele? (finden)
5. Meine Mutter _______________ eine Jacke. (finden)
6. Du _______________ einen Stuhl. (finden)

Future Tense

Saying that something occurs in the future is quite simple in German. Simply use a form of the verb **werden** (*shall*, *will*) plus an infinitive. For example:

Ich werde den Arzt anrufen. *I will call the doctor.*

Sie werden nach Hause gehen. *They will go home.*

Notice that the infinitives (**anrufen**, **gehen**) are the last elements in the previous sentences.

There is a slight irregularity in the conjugation of the verb **werden** in the second and third persons singular.

ich werde	wir werden
du **wirst**	ihr werdet
er **wird**	Sie werden
sie **wird**	sie werden
es **wird**	

Similar to English, German often uses a present-tense sentence to *imply* the future tense. This often occurs with an adverb such as **morgen** (*tomorrow*). For example:

Morgen besuche ich meinen Sohn. *Tomorrow I am visiting my son.* or *Tomorrow I will visit my son.*

Er geht morgen zur Bank. *He is going to the bank tomorrow.* or *He will go to the bank tomorrow.*

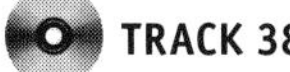

TRACK 38

Listen to the following sentences on your CD. Press "pause" to repeat each sentence. Then restate the sentence in the future tense using **werden**. Listen to the correct answer on the CD and repeat what you hear. For example:

Er geht zum Restaurant. *He goes to the restaurant.*
You say: Er wird zum Restaurant gehen. *He will go to the restaurant.*

Meine Schwester wohnt in Berlin. *My sister lives in Berlin.*

Ich kaufe eine neue Jacke. *I buy a new jacket.*

CULTURE DEMYSTIFIED

Drogerie

If you need a drugstore, look for a **Drogerie**, where you can buy hygiene products, over-the-counter medicines, and cosmetics. But there's also the **Apotheke**. There you'll often find similar products, but it's also the place where licensed pharmacists prepare prescriptions.

Sie sind zu Hause.	*They are at home.*
Wir besuchen Frau Keller.	*We visit Ms. Keller.*
Jürgen hat Sabine gern.	*Jürgen likes Sabine.*
Du hörst den Professor.	*You hear the professor.*
Tina sieht den Bahnhof.	*Tina sees the train station.*
Er ist müde.	*He is tired.*
Wir feiern meinen Geburtstag.	*We celebrate my birthday.*
Dirk geht ins Einkaufszentrum.	*Dirk goes to the shopping center.*

Written Practice 6-3

The following lines of dialogue are out of sequence. Place a number, from 1 to 6, in each blank to show the appropriate order for the lines.

_____ Gute Idee.

_____ Ja, und sie hat Fieber.

_____ Ja, sie fühlt sich nicht wohl.

_____ Ist Frau Schäfer wieder krank?

_____ Hat sie sich wieder erkältet?

_____ Wirst du sie nicht zum Arzt bringen?

PHRASES FOR SURVIVAL

Emergencies

Add these useful phrases to your language arsenal to help you get by in the German-speaking world:

Hilfe!	*Help!*
Wo ist das Krankenhaus?	*Where is the hospital?*
Ich habe Fieber.	*I have a temperature.*
Ich bin verletzt.	*I am injured.*
Es tut weh.	*It hurts.*
Ich habe Magenschmerzen.	*I have stomach pains.*

QUIZ

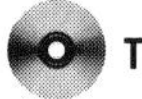
TRACK 39

Responding to questions. Listen to your CD to hear each question. Press "pause" to repeat the question out loud and select your answer—a, b, or c. Then listen to the correct answer on your CD, making sure to repeat what you hear.

1. (a) Sie geht zur Schule.
   (b) Sie ist krank.
   (c) Sie hat ihn gern.

2. (a) Er wohnt nicht hier.
   (b) Er findet einen Hut.
   (c) Er besucht seinen Vater.

3. (a) Ja, sie hat mich gern.
   (b) Nein, er ist nicht alt.
   (c) Ja, sie hat ihn gern.

4. (a) Ich weiß nicht. Ich sehe es nicht.
   (b) Ich glaube, du sollst den Arzt anrufen.
   (c) Ja, ich sehe ihn.

5. (a) Ja, er geht ins Kino.
   (b) Ja, sie ist müde.
   (c) Nein, ich werde ihn zum Arzt bringen.

Using the nouns provided as your cues, say that you see the objects (**Ich sehe ein ...**). Listen to the correct answers on your CD and repeat what you hear. For example:

die Jacke
You say: Ich sehe eine Jacke.

6. das Museum
7. der Bahnhof
8. der Zug
9. die Brücke
10. das Flugzeug

CHAPTER 7

Dining at a Restaurant

In this chapter you will learn:

- *Asking for* Bedienung *(Service)*
  - *Expressing Food Preferences Using* Gern *and* Lieber
  - *Utensils and Dishes*
- *Present Perfect Tense*

Asking for *Bedienung* (Service)

 TRACK 40

Listen to the following dialogue on your CD. After you hear a phrase or sentence on a track, always press "pause" and repeat what you hear.

CHRISTOPH: Welcher Kellner bedient an unserem Tisch?	*Which waiter is serving our table?*
TINA: Keine Ahnung. Vielleicht der junge Mann am nächsten Tisch.	*No idea. Maybe the young man at the next table.*
CHRISTOPH: Hoffentlich. Ich habe Hunger.	*I hope so. I am hungry.*
TINA: Hast du schon etwas Leckeres ausgewählt?	*Did you already choose something tasty?*
CHRISTOPH: Noch nicht. Aber dieses Restaurant ist für den Gulasch bekannt.	*Not yet. But this restaurant is known for its goulash.*
TINA: Gulasch kann fett sein. Ich möchte lieber Hähnchen mit Salat.	*Goulash can be greasy. I would rather have chicken with a salad.*
CHRISTOPH: Und zum Nachtisch?	*And for dessert?*
TINA: Vielleicht Erdbeeren mit Schlagsahne.	*Maybe strawberries with whipped cream.*
CHRISTOPH: Ich werde den Apfelstrudel probieren. Bedienung!	*I am going to try the apple strudel. Waiter!*

Dialogue Review

Answer the following questions about the dialogue Asking for **Bedienung** (Service) out loud. Cover the correct answers shown on the right. Use them to compare with your own answers.

1. Wer hat Hunger? — Christoph hat Hunger.
   Who is hungry?

2. Was kann fett sein? — Gulasch kann fett sein.
   What can be greasy?

3. Was möchte Tina lieber? — Sie möchte lieber Hähnchen mit Salat.
   What would Tina prefer to have?

4. Was möchte Tina zum Nachtisch? — Sie möchte Erdbeeren mit Schlagsahne zum Nachtisch.
   What would Tina like for dessert?

GRAMMAR DEMYSTIFIED

Some Useful New Verbs

When dining out, it is good to know the words for ordering, for consuming your food and drink, and for paying the bill. The following four verbs are just what you need: **bestellen** (*to order*), **essen** (*to eat*), **trinken** (*to drink*), and **bezahlen** (*to pay*). Notice that **essen** has a slight irregularity in the second and third persons.

Pronoun	**bestellen**	**essen**	**trinken**	**bezahlen**
ich	bestelle	esse	trinke	bezahle
du	bestellst	**isst**	trinkst	bezahlst
er, sie, es	bestellt	**isst**	trinkt	bezahlt
wir	bestellen	essen	trinken	bezahlen
ihr	bestellt	esst	trinkt	bezahlt
Sie	bestellen	essen	trinken	bezahlen
sie	bestellen	essen	trinken	bezahlen

TRACK 41

On your CD, listen to the following sentences that use the new verbs you have just learned. Press "pause" after each and repeat what you hear.

Ich möchte ein Glas Wein bestellen. — *I would like to order a glass of wine.*

Trinkst du auch Wein? — *Are you drinking wine, too?*

Er möchte ein Glas Bier bestellen. — *He would like to order a glass of beer.*

Trinkst du auch Bier? — *Do you also drink beer?*

Trinken Sie gern Sekt?	*Do you like drinking sparkling wine (champagne)?*
Nein, ich bin Antialkoholiker (-in).	*No, I am a teetotaler.*
Meine Frau isst nur vegetarisch.	*My wife eats only a vegetarian diet.*
Isst du auch nur vegetarisch?	*Do you also eat only a vegetarian diet?*
Nein, ich esse gern Schinken.	*No, I like eating ham.*
Mein Mann isst lieber Wurst.	*My husband prefers eating sausage.*
Die Kinder trinken gern Limonade.	*The children like to drink lemonade.*
Trinken Sie lieber alkoholfreie Getränke?	*Do you prefer drinking soft drinks?*
Heute bezahle ich.	*It is on me today.*
Kann ich die Rechnung in bar bezahlen?	*Can I pay the bill in cash?*

EXPRESSING FOOD PREFERENCES USING *GERN* AND *LIEBER*

The words **gern** and **lieber** come in very handy. Place one of these words after a verb to express what you *like* or what you *prefer* to do. For example:

Ich trinke gern Mineralwasser.	*I prefer to drink mineral water.*
Ich esse lieber Käse.	*I prefer to eat cheese.*
Ich höre gern Radio.	*I like to listen to the radio.*
Ich fahre lieber mit dem Zug.	*I prefer to travel by train.*

Oral Practice 7-1

TRACK 42

Listen to each of the following foods and beverages pronounced on your CD. Repeat each one as you hear it. Then ask whether *she eats* it if it is a food or whether *she drinks* it if it is a beverage. Listen to the correct answer and repeat what you hear. For example:

Bier *beer*
You say: Trinkt sie Bier? *Does she drink beer?*

Kartoffeln *potatoes*

Salat *salad*

Eier *eggs*

Schweinefleisch *pork*

Steak *steak*

Fisch *fish*

Suppe *soup*

Butter *butter*

Eis *ice cream*

Kompott *stewed fruit*

Obst *fruit*

Wasser *water*

Milch *milk*

Kaffee *coffee*

Tee *tea*

Written Practice 7-1

Using the nouns in parentheses as your cues, write sentences saying that the person referred to in each question prefers that food or beverage. For example:

Trinkst du gern Bier? (*milk*) Nein, ich trinke lieber Milch.

1. Trinkst du gern Sekt? (*wine*) ______________________________.
2. Trinkt Erik gern Limonade? (*water*) ______________________________.
3. Trinkt Sabine gern Tee? (*coffee*) ______________________________.
4. Isst du gern Wurst? (*fish*) ______________________________.
5. Isst Herr Benz gern Schinken? (*steak*) ______________________________.
6. Essen Sie gern Kartoffeln? (*salad*) ______________________________.
7. Esst ihr gern Hähnchen? (*soup*) ______________________________.
8. Isst Frau Keller gern Eier? (*fruit*) ______________________________.

9. Isst du gern Erdbeeren? (*ice cream*) ______________________.
10. Isst du gern Gulasch? (*pork*) ______________________.
11. Essen Sie gern Schlagsahne? (*butter*) ______________________.
12. Trinken Sie gern Wein? (*milk*) ______________________.

UTENSILS AND DISHES

TRACK 43

Foods and drinks are served with utensils and dishes. Listen to your CD to hear the following sentences pronounced. Press "pause" after each and repeat what you hear.

Ich hätte gern eine Tasse Kaffee bitte.	*I would like to have a cup of coffee, please.*
Gabriele hätte gern eine Tasse Tee.	*Gabriele would like a cup of tea.*
Mutti hätte gern ein Glas Orangensaft.	*Mom would like a glass of orange juice.*
Geben Sir mir bitte ein Glas Apfelsaft!	*Give me a glass of apple juice, please!*
Geben Sie uns bitte zwei Glas Rotwein!	*Give us two glasses of red wine, please!*
Geben Sie uns bitte eine Flasche Weißwein!	*Give us a bottle of white wine, please!*
Ich habe einen Teller Suppe bestellt.	*I ordered a plate (bowl) of soup.*
Er hat einen Teller Würstchen bestellt.	*He ordered a plate of sausages.*
Ich habe kein Besteck.	*I do not have any silverware.*
Ich brauche einen Löffel und ein Messer.	*I need a spoon and a knife.*
Brauchen Sie eine Gabel?	*Do you need a fork?*
Ich brauche einen Löffel Zucker.	*I need a spoonful of sugar.*

Present Perfect Tense

In English there is a tendency to relate what happened in the past by using the *simple past tense*: *I looked*, *he spoke*, or *we sang*. In spoken German, the tendency is to use the *present perfect tense*. That tense is composed of the auxiliary **haben** or **sein** plus a past participle. Most verbs use **haben** as their auxiliary. But if a verb shows motion to a place or shows a physical change or state, its auxiliary is **sein**. Many past participles require the prefix **ge-** and end with **-t**. For example:

ich habe gehört	*I have heard/I heard*
er hat gemacht	*he has made/he made*
wir haben gebraucht	*we have needed/we needed*
sie sind gereist	*they have traveled/they traveled*

If the verb has the prefix **be-**, **ent-**, **emp-**, **ge-**, **ver-**, or **zer-**, the addition of the prefix **ge-** is not required, for example: **ich habe bestellt** (*I have ordered*).

Of course, there are some irregular past participles, which come in a variety of forms. Some examples are:

Infinitive	Present Perfect Tense	
essen	ich habe gegessen	*I have eaten*
trinken	sie hat getrunken	*she has drunk*
bringen	Sie haben gebracht	*you have brought*
gehen	er ist gegangen	*he has gone*
kommen	wir sind gekommen	*we have come*
sein	du bist gewesen	*you have been*

Note that the past participle in German is the last element in a sentence: **Du bist sehr krank gewesen.** (You have been very sick.)

Check the appendix of your German dictionary or German textbook for a full list of irregular past participles.

TRACK 44

Listen to your CD to hear the following sentences pronounced. Press "pause" and repeat each one.

Ich habe noch nichts ausgewählt.	*I still have not chosen anything.*
Er hat noch nichts bestellt.	*He still has not ordered anything.*
Sie hat an unserem Tisch bedient.	*She waited on our table.*

Ich habe den Apfelstrudel probiert.	*I tried the apple strudel.*
Jürgen hat die Würstchen probiert.	*Jürgen tried the sausages.*
Wir haben den Käse probiert.	*We tried the cheese.*
Ich habe die Speisekarte gelesen.	*I read the menu.*
Hast du die Zeitung gelesen?	*Did you read the newspaper?*
Haben Sie den Brief gelesen?	*Did you read the letter?*
Haben Sie den Brief verstanden?	*Did you understand the letter?*
Wir sind nach Berlin gereist.	*We traveled to Berlin.*
Der Zug ist noch nicht angekommen.	*The train still has not arrived.*
Ich bin sehr krank gewesen.	*I have been very sick.*
Die Kellnerin ist nach Hause gegangen.	*The waitress went home.*
Der Kellner ist mit dem Bus gefahren.	*The waiter traveled by bus.*

Written Practice 7-2

Fill in each blank with the past participle of the verb in parentheses.

1. Ich habe Radio ________________ . (hören)
2. Tina hat Suppe ________________ . (bestellen)
3. Wir haben die Zeitung ________________ . (lesen)
4. Mutti ist nach Paris ________________ . (reisen)
5. Wer hat eine Gabel ________________ ? (brauchen)

Oral Practice 7-2

TRACK 45

Listen to the following questions on your CD. Press "pause" and repeat each one. Then, using the noun in parentheses as your cue, answer each question with **nein**. Listen to the correct answer, making sure to repeat what you hear. For example:

Haben Sie Suppe bestellt? (*milk*)
You say: Nein, ich habe Milch bestellt.

Haben Sie den Gulasch bestellt? (*soup*)

Haben Sie Erdbeeren ausgewählt? (*ice cream*)

Haben Sie Bier getrunken? (*wine*)

Hat er Mineralwasser getrunken? (*coffee*)

Hat sie Orangensaft getrunken? (*water*)

Habt ihr Hähnchen gegessen? (*pork*)

Hast du Salat gegessen? (*fish*)

Haben sie Limonade bestellt? (*fruit*)

Hat er Würstchen gegessen? (*stewed fruit*)

Haben Sie Sekt getrunken? (*milk*)

CULTURE DEMYSTIFIED

Konditorei

The Germans have a wonderful custom of going out for **Kaffee und Kuchen** (*coffee and cake*) in the late afternoon. Look for the sign **Konditorei** (*bakery* or *cake shop*) in any town or city and sit down to your favorite beverage and a large assortment of delicious pastries. If you don't want coffee or tea, you can always get a glass of wine or beer. Don't confuse **Konditorei** with **Bäckerei** (*bakery*), which sells breads and rolls.

Written Practice 7-3

The following lines of dialogue are out of sequence. Place a number, from 1 to 8, in each blank to show the appropriate order for the lines.

_____ Vielleicht Kompott.

_____ Sie bedient am nächsten Tisch.

_____ Dieses Restaurant ist für den Gulasch bekannt.

_____ Wo ist unsere Kellnerin?

_____ Ich weiß, aber Gulasch kann fett sein. Ich möchte lieber Salat.

_____ Ich werde das Eis probieren. Bedienung!

_____ Ich habe Hunger. Ich möchte etwas Leckeres bestellen.

_____ Und zum Nachtisch?

PHRASES FOR SURVIVAL

Dining Out

Add these useful phrases to your language arsenal to help you get by in the German-speaking world:

Zahlen bitte!	*Check please!*
Ich verstehe es nicht.	*I do not understand.*
Wie viel kostet das?	*How much does that cost?*
Das ist sehr teuer.	*That is very expensive.*
Das ist billig.	*That is cheap.*
Haben Sie eine Gedeck-Karte?	*Do you have a fixed-price menu?*
Ist Bedienung inbegriffen?	*Is service included?*
Wo sind die Toiletten?	*Where are the restrooms?*

QUIZ

TRACK 46

Responding to questions. Listen to your CD to hear each question. Press "pause" to repeat the question out loud and select your answer—a, b, or c. Then listen to the correct answer on the CD, making sure to repeat what you hear.

1. (a) Nein, du isst gern Butter.
   (b) Ja, ich trinke lieber Tee.
   (c) Ja, ich habe Hunger.

2. (a) Er bedient am nächsten Tisch.
   (b) Ich habe Erdbeeren mit Schlagsahne bestellt.
   (c) Zahlen bitte!

3. (a) Bier.
   (b) Hähnchen und Salat.
   (c) Milch.

4. (a) Nach Hause.
   (b) Ein Glas Rotwein.
   (c) Im Restaurant.

5. (a) Die Speisekarte.
   (b) Eine Gabel und einen Löffel.
   (c) Eine Flasche Bier.

Using each noun provided as your cue, say that you have ordered that item: **Ich habe ... bestellt.** Listen to the correct answers on your CD. For example:

bread
You say: Ich habe Brot bestellt.

6. *soup*
7. *ice cream*
8. *tea*
9. *potatoes*
10. *fruit*

CHAPTER 8

Going Shopping

In this chapter you will learn:

Shopping im Einkaufszentrum *(at the Mall)*

Expressing Likes Using Mir gefällt

Buying and Selling

The Idiom Es gibt

Colors

Telling Time

Shopping *im Einkaufszentrum* (at the Mall)

 TRACK 47

Listen to the following dialogue on your CD. After you hear a phrase or sentence on a track, always press "pause" and repeat what you hear.

VERKÄUFERIN: Bitte schön?	*May I help you?*
CHRISTOPH: Haben Sie diesen Pulli in dunkelblau?	*Do you have this sweater in dark blue?*
VERKÄUFERIN: Leider nicht. Ich habe ihn nur in hellblau oder grün.	*Unfortunately not. I have it only in light blue or green.*
CHRISTOPH: Schade. Er gefällt mir sehr, aber die Farbe passt nicht.	*Too bad. I really like it, but the color is not right.*
VERKÄUFERIN: Es gibt sehr schöne Hemden aus Italien in dunkelblau.	*There are very nice shirts from Italy in dark blue.*
CHRISTOPH: Nein, danke. Ich suche einen Pulli. Vielleicht bin ich zu wählerisch.	*No, thanks. I am looking for a sweater. Maybe I am too picky.*
VERKÄUFERIN: Der hellblaue Pullover ist im Ausverkauf und kostet nur zwanzig Euro.	*The light-blue sweater is on sale and costs only twenty euros.*
CHRISTOPH: Das ist aber billig. Bitte zeigen Sie mir den Hellblauen!	*That is really cheap. Show me the light-blue one, please!*
VERKÄUFERIN: Welche Größe brauchen Sie?	*What size do you need?*
CHRISTOPH: Mittelgroß.	*Medium.*

Dialogue Review

Answer the following questions about the dialogue Shopping **im Einkaufszentrum**. Cover the correct answers shown on the right. Use them to compare with your own answers.

1. Möchte Christoph ein Hemd oder einen Pulli kaufen? *Would Christoph like to buy a shirt or a sweater?*	Er möchte einen Pulli kaufen.

2. Hat die Verkäuferin einen dunkelblauen Pulli? *Does the salesperson have a dark-blue sweater?* — Nein, sie hat keinen dunkelblauen Pulli.

3. Wie viel kostet der hellblaue Pulli? *How much does the light-blue sweater cost?* — Der hellblaue Pulli kostet zwanzig Euro.

4. Ist der Pulli billig oder teuer? *Is the sweater cheap or expensive?* — Der Pulli ist billig.

EXPRESSING LIKES USING *MIR GEFÄLLT*

Another way of saying that you *like* something is with the verb **gefallen** (*to please*). But because when using this verb you are actually saying that a thing *is pleasing* or things *are pleasing* to you, the verb must be used appropriately in the singular or plural form. Sentence structure changes somewhat with the use of **gefallen**: the actual subject of the German sentence is the object of the English sentence. For example: in English one would say *I like the shirt.* The literal translation of the German sentence using **gefallen** would be: *To me is pleasing the shirt.* The object of the English sentence is *shirt*, but *shirt* (**Hemd**) is the subject of the German sentence. Practice saying these example sentences out loud:

Mir gefällt der Hut.	*I like the hat.*
Mir gefällt die Jacke.	*I like the jacket.*
Mir gefallen die Handschuhe.	*I like the gloves.*

Oral Practice 8-1

Listen to the following nouns pronounced on your CD. Press "pause" to repeat each one, and then say that *you like* that object. Listen to the correct answer and repeat what you hear. For example:

die Jacke *jacket*
You say: Mir gefällt die Jacke. *I like the jacket.*

das T-Shirt *T-shirt*

der Regenmantel *raincoat*

die Stiefel *boots*

der Schlafanzug *pajamas*

der Anzug *suit*

die Sandalen *sandals*

der Badeanzug *bathing suit*

die Windjacke *windbreaker*

die Armbanduhr *wristwatch*

die Ohrringe *earrings*

GRAMMAR DEMYSTIFIED

Using *Bitte*

The word **bitte** is used in a few different ways. Its most common meaning is *please*. For example:

Geben Sie mir bitte eine Tasse Tee!	*Please give me a cup of tea!*

But it is also used in the response to *thank you*:

Danke!/Bitte schön!	*Thanks!/You're welcome!*
Danke schön!/Bitte sehr!	*Thank you!/You're very welcome!*
Vielen Dank!/Bitte!	*Thanks a lot!/You're welcome!*

In addition, it is the customary expression a salesperson uses to ask whether you need help: **Bitte sehr?** or **Bitte schön?** (*May I help you?*) And it is often said when passing something to someone:

Hast du mal ein Tempo für mich?	*Could you give me a tissue?*
Bitte sehr! or Bitte schön!	*Here you are!*

BUYING AND SELLING

 TRACK 49

Listen to your CD to hear sentences that deal with buying and selling. Press "pause" after each sentence and repeat what you hear.

Verkaufen Sie Tabakwaren?	*Do you sell tobacco products?*
Verkaufen Sie Damenkonfektion?	*Do you sell ladies' wear?*
Gibt es hier Herrenkonfektion?	*Do you have men's clothing here?*
Gibt es hier Damenunterwäsche?	*Do you have lingerie here?*
Mein Mann hat sich neue Unterwäsche gekauft.	*My husband bought himself new underwear.*
Unser Sohn hat sich Lederhosen gekauft.	*Our son bought himself lederhosen.*
Seine Cousine hat sich eine Strumpfhose gekauft.	*His (female) cousin bought herself pantyhose.*
Ihr Cousin hat sich ein Sweatshirt gekauft.	*Her (male) cousin bought himself a sweatshirt.*
Wie viel kostet dieser Mantel?	*How much does this coat cost?*
Wie viel kostet diese Jeansjacke?	*How much does this jean jacket cost?*
Wie viel kosten diese Strümpfe?	*How much do these stockings cost?*
Wie viel kosten diese Turnschuhe?	*How much do these gym shoes cost?*

THE IDIOM *ES GIBT*

The phrase **es gibt** is used idiomatically to mean *there is* or *there are*. Practice saying out loud the following sentences that illustrate the use of this important idiom:

Gibt es Kaffee zum Frühstück?	*Is there coffee for breakfast?*
Nein, es gibt keinen Kaffee.	*No, there is no coffee.*
Gibt es Hähnchen zum Mittagessen?	*Is there chicken for lunch?*
Nein, es gibt nur Suppe.	*No, there is only soup.*
Was gibt es zum Abendessen?	*What is for supper?*
Zum Abendessen gibt es Sauerbraten.	*There is sauerbraten for supper.*

Oral Practice 8-2

TRACK 50

Listen to your CD to hear the following questions. Press "pause" to repeat each question. Then, using the noun in parentheses as your cue, answer that the person in the question *has on* that item of clothing. Cover the correct answers shown on the right. Use them to compare with your own answers. For example:

Hat Sabine eine Bluse an? (Kleid) *You say*: Nein, sie hat ein Kleid an.	*Does Sabine have a blouse on?* *No, she has a dress on.*
Hat Mutti eine Armbanduhr an? (Ohrringe)	Nein, sie hat Ohrringe an.
Hat Karl einen Regenmantel an? (Anzug)	Nein, er hat einen Anzug an.
Hat Christoph einen Pulli an? (T-Shirt)	Nein, er hat ein T-Shirt an.
Hat Renate Stiefel an? (Sandalen)	Nein, sie hat Sandalen an.
Hat Werner eine Jacke an? (Windjacke)	Nein, er hat eine Windjacke an.
Hat Tina einen Rock an? (Schlafanzug)	Nein, sie hat einen Schlafanzug an.
Hat Erik ein Hemd an? (Badeanzug)	Nein, er hat einen Badeanzug an.
Hat Angela Ohrringe an? (Armbanduhr)	Nein, sie hat eine Armbanduhr an.
Hat Herr Benz einen Anzug an? (Regenmantel)	Nein, er hat einen Regenmantel an.
Hat Frau Keller Schuhe an? (Stiefel)	Nein, sie hat Stiefel an.

GRAMMAR DEMYSTIFIED

The Verb *Tragen*

The verb **anhaben** means *to have clothing on*. But another verb that can be used in its place is **tragen** (*to wear, to carry*). For example:

Ich trage ein neues Hemd.	*I am wearing a new shirt.*
Du trägst einen alten Hut.	*You are wearing an old hat.*
Sie trägt einen blauen Rock.	*She is wearing a blue skirt.*
Wir tragen keine Schuhe.	*We are not wearing any shoes.*
Ihr tragt braune Sandalen.	*You are wearing brown sandals.*
Sie tragen meinen Pulli.	*You are wearing my sweater.*

COLORS

TRACK 51

Listen to your CD to hear sentences that deal with colors. Press "pause" after each sentence and repeat what you hear.

Mein neuer Pulli ist braun.	*My new sweater is brown.*
Diese Hose ist schwarz.	*These pants are black.*
Ihre Strumpfhose ist weiß.	*Her pantyhose are white.*
Dieses Hemd ist rot.	*This shirt is red.*
Ist dein Badeanzug blau oder grün?	*Is your bathing suit blue or green?*
Karl trägt einen schwarzen Mantel.	*Karl is wearing a black coat.*
Tina kauft eine weiße Bluse.	*Tina buys a white blouse.*

Herr Keller verkauft den roten VW.	*Mr. Keller sells the red VW.*
Sabine hat ein grünes Kleid an.	*Sabine has a green dress on.*
Ich möchte einen braunen Regenmantel.	*I would like a brown raincoat.*
Wer hat den blauen Anzug gekauft?	*Who bought the blue suit?*
Wer hat die schwarzen Stiefel verkauft?	*Who sold the black boots?*

GRAMMAR DEMYSTIFIED

Adjectives

When adjectives, such as colors, are used as predicate adjectives in German, they have no endings. But when they modify a noun directly, these adjectives require endings. For example:

Predicate Adjectives	**Modifying Adjectives**
Mein Wagen ist rot.	Ich habe einen roten Wagen.
Die Stiefel sind schwarz.	Ich habe die schwarzen Stiefel gekauft.
Der Hut ist neu.	Ich kaufe einen neuen Hut.

Oral Practice 8-3

 TRACK 52

Listen to your CD to hear the following questions. Press "pause" to repeat each question. Then, using the word in parentheses as your cue, answer in the negative. Cover the correct answers shown on the right. Use them to compare with your own answers. For example:

Kaufen Sie einen Hut? (*gloves*) *You say*: Nein, ich kaufe Handschuhe.	*Are you buying a hat?* *No, I am buying gloves.*

Kaufen Sie einen Rock? (*dress*)	Nein, ich kaufe ein Kleid.
Kauft er ein rotes Hemd? (*windbreaker*)	Nein, er kauft eine rote Windjacke.

Kauft sie eine blaue Jacke? (*bathing suit*)	Nein, sie kauft einen blauen Badeanzug.
Hast du einen neuen Mantel an? (*suit*)	Nein, ich habe einen neuen Anzug an.
Habt ihr alte Schuhe an? (*sandals*)	Nein, wir haben alte Sandalen an.
Hat er eine Windjacke an? (*raincoat*)	Nein, er hat einen Regenmantel an.
Tragen Sie schwarze Schuhe? (*boots*)	Nein, ich trage schwarze Stiefel.
Trägt sie eine weiße Bluse? (*jacket*)	Nein, sie trägt eine weiße Jacke.
Trägst du eine Armbanduhr? (*earrings*)	Nein, ich trage Ohrringe.
Verkaufst du Schuhe? (*gloves*)	Nein, ich verkaufe Handschuhe.

GRAMMAR DEMYSTIFIED

Possessive Adjectives

Each of the German pronouns has a *possessive adjective form* just as the English pronouns do. And like German definite articles, the possessive adjectives reflect the gender of the nouns they modify. Therefore, feminine and plural possessive adjectives will end in **-e**, and masculine possessive adjectives that modify a direct object (which requires the accusative case) will end in **-en**.

Pronoun	**Masculine and Neuter/Feminine or Plural/Masculine Accusative**	
ich	mein/meine/meinen	*my, mine*
du	dein/deine/deinen	*your, yours*
er	sein/seine/seinen	*his*
sie	ihr/ihre/ihren	*her, hers*
es	sein/seine/seinen	*its*
wir	unser/unsere/unseren	*our, ours*
ihr	euer/eure/euren	*your, yours*
Sie	Ihr/Ihre/Ihren	*your, yours*
sie	ihr/ihre/ihren	*their, theirs*

Written Practice 8-1

TRACK 53

Listen to your CD to hear each of the following sentences. Using the cue words in parentheses, rewrite each sentence. Then listen to the correct answers on your CD and repeat what you hear. For example:

Erik hat deinen Hut. (mein) *Erik hat meinen Hut.*

1. Sie hat deine Bluse an. (mein) ____________________.
2. Ich trage dein rotes Hemd. (sein) ____________________.
3. Sabine kauft unseren Wagen. (euer) ____________________.
4. Verkaufst du ihre Ohrringe? (dein) ____________________.
5. Verkaufen Sie meinen Rock? (Ihr) ____________________.
6. Dein Anzug gefällt mir sehr. (sein) ____________________.
7. Ihre Lehrerin ist zu Hause. (unser) ____________________.
8. Mein Kleid ist sehr teuer. (ihr) ____________________.
9. Er wird unseren VW kaufen. (mein) ____________________.
10. Sie trägt meine Jacke. (sein) ____________________.

Written Practice 8-2

Fill in each blank with the appropriate form of the possessive adjective in parentheses (masculine, feminine, neuter, or plural).

1. ____________ Sandalen sind sehr alt. (mein)
2. ____________ Schule ist in Berlin. (unser)
3. Wo wohnt ____________ Bruder? (Ihr)
4. ____________ Großmutter versteht kein Deutsch. (sein)
5. Wer hat ____________ Kleid gekauft? (dein)

CULTURE DEMYSTIFIED

Money

To change money in a German-speaking country, the obvious place to go is **die Bank**. But also look for signs with the words **Sparkasse** (*savings bank*) and **Geldwechsel** or **Wechselstube** (*currency exchange office*).

The **Euro** is now the standard currency of most of Europe, including Germany. Just like a dollar, one **Euro** consists of **hundert Cent** (*100 cents*). Be sure to check the **Wechselkurs** to learn the latest *rate of exchange*. And to find an ATM, look for the word **Geldautomat**. The following words regarding money will come in handy:

das Geld	*money*
die Reiseschecks	*traveler's checks*
die Kreditkarte	*credit card*

Written Practice 8-3

The following lines of dialogue are out of sequence. Place a number, from 1 to 8, in each blank to show the appropriate order for the lines.

______ Ja, wir haben Hemden und Hosen aus Rom.

______ Nein, danke. Blau geht nicht. Haben Sie schwarze Hosen?

______ Ich möchte ein grünes Hemd.

______ Bitte schön?

______ Das ist sehr billig.

______ Haben Sie Herrenkonfektion aus Italien?

______ Hemden in grün haben wir leider nicht. Möchten Sie blau?

______ Ja, schwarz haben wir, und sie kosten nur zwanzig Euro.

Telling Time

German uses the twenty-four-hour clock when telling time and therefore does not use A.M. and P.M. Practice reading the following sentences out loud.

Wie viel Uhr ist es?	*What time is it?*
Es ist ein Uhr.	*It is one o'clock* A.M.
Es ist dreizehn Uhr.	*It is one o'clock* P.M.
Es ist sechs Uhr.	*It is six o'clock* A.M.
Es ist zwanzig Uhr.	*It is eight o'clock* P.M.
Es ist Viertel nach drei.	*It is three fifteen* A.M.
Es ist achtzehn Uhr fünfzehn.	*It is six fifteen* P.M.
Es ist halb neun.	*It is eight thirty* A.M.
Es ist dreiundzwanzig Uhr dreißig.	*It is eleven thirty* P.M.
Es ist Viertel vor zehn.	*It is a quarter to ten* A.M.
Es ist neunzehn Uhr fünfundvierzig.	*It is a quarter to eight* P.M.

Oral Practice 8-4

TRACK 54

Look at the following times provided in English. Translate each one out loud into German; then listen to your CD to hear the correct answers, making sure to repeat what you hear. For example:

3:30 A.M.
You say: Es ist halb vier.

2:00 A.M.

2:00 P.M.

5:15 A.M.

9:15 P.M.

4:30 A.M.

11:30 P.M.

1:45 A.M.

7:45 P.M.

8:30 A.M.

10:00 P.M.

PHRASES FOR SURVIVAL

A Little Shopping Trip

Add these useful phrases to your language arsenal to help you get by in the German-speaking world:

Wo kann ich einen Regenschirm kaufen?	*Where can I buy an umbrella?*
Ich möchte ein Paar Stiefel.	*I would like a pair of boots.*
Können Sie bitte meine Masse nehmen?	*Can you measure me, please?*
Wo kann ich es anprobieren?	*Where can I try it on?*

QUIZ

TRACK 55

Responding to questions. Listen to your CD to hear each question. Press "pause" to repeat the question out loud and select your answer—a, b, or c. Then listen to the correct answer on the CD, making sure to repeat what you hear.

1. (a) Es ist vier Uhr.
   (b) Vierzig Euro.
   (c) Das ist billig.

2. (a) Ein rotes Kleid.
   (b) Dunkelblau.
   (c) Unser neuer VW.

3. (a) Das Hemd gefällt mir sehr.
   (b) Er kauft einen schönen Anzug.
   (c) Sie verkaufen ihren Wagen.

4. (a) Nein, das ist meine neue Windjacke.
   (b) Ja, der Regenmantel ist alt.
   (c) Nein, es ist teuer.

5. (a) Sie haben Hemden aus Italien.
   (b) Sie trägt schwarze Stiefel.
   (c) Ich trage ein weißes Sweatshirt.

Using the words provided as your cues, say that Erik has bought each object: **Erik hat ... gekauft.** Listen to the correct answers on your CD. For example:

Jacke
You say: Erik hat eine Jacke gekauft.

6. Badeanzug
7. Ohrringe
8. Sandalen
9. Regenmantel
10. Armbanduhr

CHAPTER 9

Traveling by Train

In this chapter you will learn:

Am Bahnhof (at the Train Station)

TRACK 56

Listen to the following dialogue on your CD. After you hear a phrase or sentence on a track, always press "pause" and repeat what you hear.

HERR BENZ: Hier ist der Eingang. Mach schnell! Wir müssen noch Fahrkarten lösen.	*Here is the entrance. Hurry up! We still have to buy the tickets.*
FRAU BENZ: Wir hätten sie vorgestern im Reisebüro kaufen sollen. Ich habe gesagt ...	*We should have bought them the day before yesterday at the travel agency. I said . . .*
HERR BENZ: Ja, ja. Du hast immer recht. Beeil dich!	*Yes, yes. You are always right. Hurry!*
FRAU BENZ: Ich kann nicht schneller laufen. Mein Koffer ist zu schwer.	*I cannot go any faster. My suitcase is too heavy.*
HERR BENZ: Wenn du meinen Rucksack nimmst, kann ich den Koffer für dich tragen.	*If you take my backpack, I can carry your suitcase for you.*
FRAU BENZ: Danke. Der Rucksack ist viel leichter. Hier ist der Schalter.	*Thanks. The backpack is a lot lighter. Here is the ticket window.*
HERR BENZ: Bitte zwei Rückfahrkarten nach Salzburg. Zweiter Klasse.	*Two round-trip tickets to Salzburg, please. Second class.*
FRAU BENZ: Auf welchem Gleis fährt der Zug ab?	*On what track does the train depart?*
HERR BENZ: Auf Gleis drei. Dort drüben.	*On track three. Over there.*
SCHAFFNER: Einsteigen bitte!	*Conductor: All aboard, please!*

Dialogue Review

Answer the following questions about the dialogue **Am Bahnhof**. Cover the correct answers shown on the right. Use them to compare with your own answers.

1. Was muss Herr Benz noch lösen? *What does Mr. Benz still have to buy?*	Er muss die Fahrkarten noch lösen.
2. Was ist zu schwer? *What is too heavy?*	Der Koffer ist zu schwer.
3. Wohin reisen sie? *Where are they traveling?*	Sie reisen nach Salzburg.
4. Wer sagt, „Einsteigen bitte"? *Who says, "All aboard, please"?*	Der Schaffner sagt, „Einsteigen bitte".

Giving Commands with Imperatives

Imperatives are verbs in the command form. Since commands are given to the second person singular and plural (*you*), German has three imperative forms: one each for **du**, **ihr**, and **Sie**. These three imperative forms are used for informal or formal relationships as dictated by the pronouns **du**, **ihr**, and **Sie**. The imperative forms look like this:

du-*command*: Mach schnell!	*Hurry up!*
ihr-*command*: Macht schnell!	*Hurry up!*
Sie-*command*: Machen Sie schnell!	*Hurry up!*

Naturally, by adding **bitte** (*please*) to a command, it sounds more courteous: **Machen Sie bitte schnell!** (*Please hurry up!*)

Most verbs as imperatives follow the patterns of **du**, **ihr**, and **Sie** as illustrated above. But if a verb has a vowel change from **e** to **i** or **ie** in the second person singular conjugation, that irregularity occurs in the imperative also. Let's look at some examples:

Infinitive	**e → i or ie**	**du**	**ihr**	**Sie**
helfen	du hilfst	Hilf!	Helft!	Helfen Sie! (*Help!*)
geben	du gibst	Gib!	Gebt!	Geben Sie! (*Give!*)
sehen	du siehst	Sieh!	Seht!	Sehen Sie! (*See!*)
stehlen	du stiehlst	Stiehl!	Stehlt!	Stehlen Sie! (*Steal!*)

The verb **sein** is a special case. Take note of its imperative forms:

Infinitive	**du**	**ihr**	**Sie**
sein	Sei!	Seid!	Seien Sie! (*Be!*)

In written form, a German imperative is always followed by an exclamation point: **Beeil dich!** (*Hurry!*)

Oral Practice 9-1

TRACK 57

Listen to your CD to hear imperative sentences given in the **du**-command form. Press "pause" after each sentence and repeat what you hear. Then restate the sentence as a **Sie**-command. Press "pause" to hear each correct answer, making sure to repeat what you hear. For example:

Trag meinen Koffer! *Carry my suitcase!*
You say: Tragen Sie meinen Koffer!

Kauf eine Flasche Wein!	*Buy a bottle of wine.*
Sei mein Freund!	*Be my friend.*
Trink ein Glas Milch!	*Drink a glass of milk.*
Geh bitte nach Hause!	*Please go home!*
Zeig mir bitte den Pulli!	*Please show me the sweater.*
Lös die Fahrkarten!	*Buy the tickets.*
Sprich Deutsch!	*Speak German!*
Bestell den Gulasch!	*Order the goulash.*
Bezahl bitte in bar!	*Please pay in cash!*
Fahr mit dem Zug!	*Go by train.*
Gib mir ein Glas Rotwein!	*Give me a glass of red wine.*
Lies bitte die Speisekarte!	*Please read the menu.*
Glaub mir!	*Believe me.*
Ruf den Arzt an!	*Phone the doctor.*
Besuch Frau Keller!	*Visit Ms. Keller.*

Modal Auxiliaries

There are a few important verbs used to modify the meaning of the verbs they accompany. These are called *modal auxiliaries*. The five most commonly used modal auxiliaries are **dürfen** (*may, to be allowed*), **können** (*can, to be able*), **müssen** (*must, to have to*), **sollen** (*should, to be supposed to*), and **wollen** (*to want*). You've already encountered some of these verbs in the dialogues. For example:

Ich will ihn zum Arzt bringen.	*I want to take him to the doctor.*
Wir müssen die Fahrkarten lösen.	*We have to buy the tickets.*
Ich kann nicht schneller laufen.	*I cannot walk any faster.*

PRESENT TENSE OF MODALS

The modal auxiliaries have a special conjugation that is a bit different from other verbs.

Pronoun	**dürfen**	**können**	**müssen**	**sollen**	**wollen**
ich	darf	kann	muss	soll	will
du	darfst	kannst	musst	sollst	willst
er, sie, es	darf	kann	muss	soll	will
wir	dürfen	können	müssen	sollen	wollen
ihr	dürft	könnt	müsst	sollt	wollt
Sie	dürfen	können	müssen	sollen	wollen
sie	dürfen	können	müssen	sollen	wollen

Modal auxiliaries are most often accompanied by any one of a large variety of infinitives, which are placed as the last element in a sentence. Practice saying out loud the following sentences that illustrate the use of modal auxiliaries:

Darf ich bitten?	*May I have this dance?*
Meine Freundin darf nicht mitkommen.	*My girlfriend may not come along.*
Können Sie kochen?	*Can you cook?*
Sie kann es nur mit einer Brille lesen.	*She can only read it with her glasses on.*

Muss er zu Hause bleiben?	*Does he have to stay home?*
Sie müssen einen Ausweis haben.	*You must have an ID.*
Soll ich die Pillen jeden Tag einnehmen?	*Should I take the pills every day?*
Ihr sollt sofort damit aufhören!	*You should stop that immediately!*
Will Erik ein Dichter sein?	*Does Erik want to be a poet?*
Wir wollen die Stadt besichtigen.	*We want to go sightseeing in the city.*

GRAMMAR DEMYSTIFIED

Mögen

The verb **mögen** is a modal auxiliary used in some special ways. When used alone, it means *to like*.

Ich mag Erdbeeren mit Schlagsahne.	*I like strawberries with whipped cream.*
Sabine mag keine Tulpen.	*Sabine does not like tulips.*

When **mögen** is used with another verb in its infinitive form, it means *may*.

Das mag sein.	*That may be (the case).*
Er mag krank werden.	*He may get sick.*

Another very common usage of this verb is in its subjunctive form **möchte** (*would like*). This form is often used in place of **wollen** to sound more polite.

Möchten Sie ein Glas Sekt?	*Would you like a glass of champagne?*
Ich möchte den Sauerbraten bestellen.	*I would like to order the sauerbraten.*

Oral Practice 9-2

 **TRACK 58**

Listen to each of the following nouns pronounced on your CD. Press "pause" after each noun and repeat what you hear. Then ask whether you can see that object. Listen to the correct question on the CD, making sure to repeat it out loud. For example:

> die Schule *school*
> *You say:* Kannst du die Schule sehen?

die Stadt *city*

das Dorf *village*

der Hafen *harbor*

die Universität *university*

der Zoo *zoo*

die Berge *mountains*

der Fluss *river*

der See *lake*

SOME USEFUL NEW WORDS

You have encountered numerous new verbs that can be used with a variety of useful nouns. Chapter 5 addressed the use of the phrase **ist ... geboren** (*was born*) together with dates and months. But the same phrase can be accompanied by seasons. For example:

Wann ist dein Sohn geboren? Mein Sohn ist im Winter geboren.	*When was your son born? My son was born in the winter.*
Wann ist deine Tochter geboren? Meine Tochter ist im Frühling geboren.	*When was your daughter born? My daughter was born in the spring.*

Wann ist sein Vater geboren? Sein Vater ist im Sommer geboren.	*When was his father born? His father was born in the summer.*
Wann ist eure Mutter geboren? Unsere Mutter ist im Herbst geboren.	*When was your mother born? Our mother was born in the fall.*

Oral Practice 9-3

Similar to the verb phrase previously illustrated, the following verbs already familiar to you can be used with many new nouns. This exercise will give you some practice with this concept. Read each question out loud. Then, using the noun in parentheses as your cue, answer that someone is *photographing* that object. Cover the correct answers shown on the right. Use them to compare with your own answers. For example:

Was fotografiert Sabine? (*museum*) *You say*: Sabine fotografiert das Museum.	*Sabine is photographing the museum.*

Was fotografiert Werner? (*zoo*)	Werner fotografiert den Zoo.
Was fotografiert deine Freundin? (*village*)	Meine Freundin fotografiert das Dorf.
Was fotografieren Sie? (*university*)	Ich fotografiere die Universität.
Was fotografiert ihr? (*harbor*)	Wir fotografieren den Hafen.
Was fotografieren Sie? (*river*)	Ich fotografiere den Fluss.
Was fotografiert Gabi? (*lake*)	Gabi fotografiert den See.
Was fotografiert Ihr Vater? (*city*)	Mein Vater fotografiert die Stadt.
Was fotografiert Jürgen? (*mountains*)	Jürgen fotografiert die Berge.

The following questions ask what someone *likes*. Answer each question saying that the person likes what's indicated by the noun in parentheses. Cover the correct answers shown on the right. Use them to compare with your own answers. For example:

Was mag Christoph? (*coffee*) *You say*: Christoph mag Kaffee.	*Christoph likes coffee.*

Was mag Herr Keller? (*pork*)	Herr Keller mag Schweinefleisch.
Was mögen die Kinder? (*ice cream*)	Die Kinder mögen Eis.
Was magst du? (*salad*)	Ich mag Salat.
Was mögt ihr? (*fruit*)	Wir mögen Obst.
Was mögen deine Eltern? (*tea*)	Meine Eltern mögen Tee.

The following questions ask what someone *sees*. Answer each question saying that the person sees what's indicated by the noun in parentheses. Cover the correct answers shown on the right. Use them to compare with your own answers. For example:

Was sieht Astrid? (*jacket*)
You say: Astrid sieht die Jacke. *Astrid sees the jacket.*

Was sehen Sie? (*zoo*)	Ich sehe den Zoo.
Was sieht Frau Benz? (*movie theater*)	Frau Benz sieht das Kino.
Was sehen deine Eltern? (*university*)	Meine Eltern sehen die Universität.
Was sieht Tina? (*wristwatch*)	Tina sieht die Armbanduhr.
Was siehst du? (*train station*)	Ich sehe den Bahnhof.

Oral Practice 9-4

TRACK 59

Listen to your CD to hear each of the following sentences. Press "pause" to repeat what you hear. Then, using the modal auxiliary in parentheses, restate the sentence. Then listen to the correct answer on your CD, making sure to repeat what you hear. For example:

Erik kauft einen Hut. (wollen)
You say: Erik will einen Hut kaufen.

Sie kauft eine Bluse. (wollen)

Ich spreche nur Deutsch. (müssen)

Wir hören Radio. (wollen)

Helft ihr Frau Schneider? (können)

Er löst die Fahrkarten. (sollen)

Sie kommen nicht mit. (dürfen)

Laufen Sie schneller? (können)

Sie fährt mit dem Zug. (müssen)

Trägst du den Koffer? (können)

Erik verkauft den VW. (sollen)

Er kauft den VW. (möchte)

Wir reisen nach Heidelberg. (möchte)

Ich bestelle Erdbeeren. (möchte)

Sie bleibt zu Hause. (möchte)

Werner ist ein Dichter. (möchte)

SAYING WHAT ONE SHOULD OR SHOULD NOT HAVE DONE

There is a very useful phrase to employ when there are doubts about something that has just occurred. This phrase uses the modal auxiliary **sollen** preceded by an infinitive. Practice saying the following sentences out loud:

Das hättest du nicht tun sollen!	*You should not have done that!*
Das hättest du nicht sagen sollen!	*You should not have said that!*
Das hätten wir nicht kaufen sollen!	*We should not have bought that!*
Das hätten Sie nicht essen sollen!	*You should not have eaten that!*
Das hätte ich nicht trinken sollen!	*I should not have drunk that!*
Das hätte er nicht verkaufen sollen!	*He should not have sold that!*

Making Comparisons

Comparatives are relatively simple but extremely useful forms of adjectives and adverbs. To construct the comparative forms in German—just as in English—simply add the suffix **-er** to an adjective or adverb. For example:

Positive Form	Comparative Form	
klein	kleiner	*smaller*
leicht	leichter	*lighter, easier*
neu	neuer	*newer*
schnell	schneller	*faster*
schwer	schwerer	*heavier*

If an adjective or adverb has an umlaut vowel, there is a tendency to add an umlaut to its comparative form: **jung—jünger** (*younger*), **alt—älter** (*older*). And like in English, there are a few irregular comparative forms:

Positive Form	Comparative Form	
bald	eher	*sooner*
groß	größer	*bigger*
gut	besser	*better*
hoch	höher	*higher*
nah	näher	*nearer*

The word **als** (*than*) is used to compare two things: **Italien ist kleiner als Deutschland.** (*Italy is smaller than Germany.*) **Tina schreibt besser als Werner.** (*Tina writes better than Werner.*)

Oral Practice 9-5

TRACK 60

Listen to your CD to hear each of the following sentences. Press "pause" to repeat each sentence, and then, using the word in parentheses, restate the sentence using a comparative. Then listen to the correct answer on your CD, making sure to repeat what you hear. For example:

Tina ist klein. (Sabine)
You say: Tina ist kleiner als Sabine.

Erik ist groß. (Christoph)

Die Stiefel sind neu. (Sandalen)

Das Hotel ist hoch. (Museum)

Anna ist schön. (Katrin)

Meine Mutter ist jung. (mein Vater)

Dein Koffer ist leicht. (mein Koffer)

Unser Wagen ist billig. (euer Wagen)

Karl lernt gut. (sein Bruder)

Renate spricht schnell. (ihre Schwester)

Der Bus kommt bald. (der Zug)

Written Practice 9-1

Fill in each blank with the comparative form of the adjective or adverb shown in parentheses.

1. Mein Wagen ist _______________ . (billig)
2. Ist Werner _______________ als Thomas? (alt)
3. Meine Freundin ist viel _______________ . (schön)
4. Martin läuft _______________ als Christoph. (schnell)
5. Ist das _______________ ? (gut)

VOCABULARY DEMYSTIFIED

Border Crossing

When crossing the border into Germany, one encounters the **Grenzpolizei** (*border police*). The border (**die Grenze**) is where you'll also see the sign **Zoll** (*customs*). At the border a variety of things might be checked. For example:

der Pass	*passport*
die Fahrkarte	*ticket*
die Versicherungskarte	*insurance certificate*
der Führerschein	*driver's license*
der Ausweis	*identification*

In addition, you'll probably hear the question: **Haben Sie etwas zu verzollen?** (*Do you have anything to declare?*)

Written Practice 9-2

The following lines of dialogue are out of sequence. Place a number, from 1 to 8, in each blank to show the appropriate order for the lines.

______ Auf welchem Gleis fährt der Zug ab?

______ Mein Koffer ist zu schwer.

______ Du hättest sie vorgestern im Reisebüro kaufen sollen.

______ Ja, vielleicht. Warum gehst du nicht schneller?

______ Ich kann den Koffer für dich tragen.

______ Beeil dich! Da ist der Schalter. Ich muss die Fahrkarten noch lösen.

______ Einsteigen bitte!

______ Auf Gleis eins. Dort drüben.

PHRASES FOR SURVIVAL

Transportation

Add these useful phrases to your language arsenal to help you get by in the German-speaking world:

Man kann Fahrkarten in Reisebüros kaufen.	*You can buy tickets in travel agencies.*
Unser Bus fährt um 14 Uhr 20 ab.	*Our bus departs at 2:20 P.M.*
Der Zug kommt um 9 Uhr in Berlin an.	*The train arrives at 9 A.M. in Berlin.*
Hier müssen wir umsteigen.	*We have to transfer here.*
An der Ecke wollen wir aussteigen.	*We want to get off at the corner.*
An der Bushaltestelle können wir einsteigen.	*We can get on at the bus stop.*

QUIZ

Responding to questions. Listen to your CD to hear each question. Press "pause" to repeat the question out loud and select your answer—a, b, or c. Then listen to the correct answer on the CD, making sure to repeat what you hear.

1. (a) Es ist halb neun. Mach schnell!
   (b) Da ist der Schalter.
   (c) Geben Sie mir die Fahrkarten!

2. (a) Nein, sein Koffer ist zu Hause.
   (b) Der Zug fährt schneller.
   (c) Nein, er ist sehr leicht.

3. (a) Ja, ich muss in der Stadt bleiben.
   (b) Nein, sprechen Sie bitte Englisch!
   (c) Ja, wir wollen zwei Glas Wein bestellen.

4. (a) Nein, ich möchte lieber einen Salat.
   (b) Bitte schön!
   (c) Beeil dich!

5. (a) Ja, Sabine ist jünger als Thomas.
   (b) Nein, mein Vater ist nicht jung.
   (c) Ja, das ist viel besser.

Using the word provided as your cue, say that you have visited that place: **Ich habe ... besucht.** Listen to the correct answers on your CD, making sure to repeat what you hear. For example:

library
You say: Ich habe die Bibliothek besucht.

6. *zoo*
7. *university*
8. *city*
9. *harbor*
10. *village*

CHAPTER 10

A Trip to the Beach

In this chapter you will learn:

Planning der Ausflug *(the Outing)*

Talking About the Weather

Weather-Related Activities

Using Superlatives

Planning *der Ausflug* (the Outing)

 **TRACK 1**

Listen to the following dialogue on your CD. After you hear a phrase or sentence on a track, always press "pause" and repeat what you hear.

STEFAN: Warum schläfst du noch? Es ist schon halb acht.	*Why are you still sleeping? It is already seven thirty.*

ANDREA: Ich kann nicht aufstehen. Ich bin noch müde.	*I cannot get up. I am still tired.*
STEFAN: Aber die Kinder warten in der Küche. Sie wollen Frühstück.	*But the children are waiting in the kitchen. They want breakfast.*
ANDREA: Schon gut. Ich stehe auf. Wie ist das Wetter?	*All right. I will get up. How is the weather?*
STEFAN: Perfekt. Zweiundzwanzig Grad und sonnig.	*Perfect. Twenty-two degrees and sunny.*
ANDREA: Schön. Fahren wir mit der Straßenbahn zum Strand?	*Fine. Are we going to the beach by streetcar?*
STEFAN: Nein. Das dauert zu lange. Wir nehmen den Zug.	*No. That takes too long. We will take the train.*
ANDREA: Aber der Bahnhof ist ziemlich weit von hier entfernt.	*But the station is rather far from here.*
STEFAN: Macht nichts! Ich habe schon angerufen. In dreißig Minuten kommt ein Taxi.	*It does not matter. I already phoned. A taxi will be here in thirty minutes.*

Dialogue Review

Answer the following questions about the dialogue Planning **der Ausflug**. Cover the correct answers shown on the right. Use them to compare with your own answers.

1. Wer schläft noch? *Who is still sleeping?*	Andrea schläft noch.
2. Wo sind die Kinder? *Where are the children?*	Die Kinder sind in der Küche.
3. Ist das Wetter gut oder schlecht? *Is the weather good or bad?*	Das Wetter ist gut.

4. Wie fahren sie zum Strand? Sie fahren mit dem Zug.
   How are they getting to the beach?

5. Ist der Bahnhof nah oder weit? Der Bahnhof ist weit.
   Is the train station near or far?

TALKING ABOUT THE WEATHER

The phrase used to ask about the weather in German is: **Wie ist das Wetter?** *How is the weather?* As in many places, the weather is often a topic of conversation in the German-speaking world. When describing weather-related conditions, German does what English does: it refers to the weather as *it*—**es**. Practice saying out loud the following sentences that refer to the weather:

Es ist kalt.	*It is cold.*
Es ist heiß.	*It is hot.*
Es ist warm gewesen.	*It was warm.*
Es ist gestern kühl gewesen.	*It was cool yesterday.*
Es wird regnerisch sein.	*It is going to be rainy.*
Es wird morgen neblig sein.	*It is going to be foggy tomorrow.*
Es regnet.	*It is raining.*
Es schneit.	*It is snowing.*
Es ist windig.	*It is windy.*
Es blizt und donnert.	*There is lightning and thunder.*
Es ist stürmisch.	*It is stormy.*
Es ist wolkig.	*It is cloudy.*
Es ist schönes Wetter.	*The weather is fine/nice.*

Oral Practice 10-1

TRACK 2

Listen to your CD to hear questions regarding weather. Press "pause" to repeat each question after you hear it. Then answer the question with **nein**, using the cue word in parentheses and the adverb **wieder** (*again*). Listen to the correct answer on your CD, making sure to repeat what you hear. For example:

Ist es kalt? (warm)	*Is it cold?*
You say: Nein, es ist wieder warm.	*No, it is warm again.*

Ist es stürmisch? (sonnig)

Ist es kühl? (warm)

Ist es neblig? (wolkig)

Ist es heiß? (windig)

Regnet es? (schneit)

Blitzt es? (regnet)

Schneit es? (schönes Wetter)

Ist es warm? (kühl)

Donnert es? (neblig)

Ist es sonnig? (regnerisch)

WEATHER-RELATED ACTIVITIES

TRACK 3

Good weather is relative. A lot depends upon whether you're a beachcomber or a ski enthusiast. To ask in German what one likes to do in good weather, say: **Was macht man bei schönem Wetter?** *What do you do in good weather?* Let's look at some weather-related activities that might be used in a response to this question. Listen to your CD and practice saying the following sentences:

Am Strand spielen wir Volleyball.	*At the beach we play volleyball.*
Am Strand geht unsere Familie fischen.	*Our family goes fishing at the beach.*

Am Strand werde ich sonnenbaden.	*I am going to sunbathe at the beach.*
Am Strand gehen die Kinder schwimmen.	*At the beach the children go swimming.*
Im Wald wandern wir.	*We hike in the woods.*
Im Wald sammelt Gabi Pilze.	*Gabi gathers mushrooms in the woods.*
Im Wald fotografiert Erik die Vögel.	*Erik photographs birds in the woods.*
Im Wald geht mein Onkel oft jagen.	*My uncle often goes hunting in the woods.*
In den Bergen gehen wir oft klettern.	*We often go climbing in the mountains.*
In den Bergen haben wir eine Hütte.	*We have a cabin in the mountains.*
In den Bergen kann man Hirsche sehen.	*You can see deer in the mountains.*
In den Bergen sitzen wir um das Lagerfeuer.	*We sit around the campfire in the mountains.*

It is very common to use the verb **gehen** (*to go*) to describe an activity. In this kind of structure, the verb **gehen** is conjugated, and the sentence ends with an infinitive. For example:

Ich gehe morgen jagen.	*I am going hunting tomorrow.*
Die Jungen gehen schwimmen.	*The boys are going swimming.*

Oral Practice 10-2

TRACK 4

Use the verb provided to say that *they are going to take part in that activity with us tomorrow.* Cover the correct answers shown on the right, listen to the correct answers on the CD, and repeat what you hear. Use them to compare with your own answers. For example:

schwimmen	*to swim*
You say: Morgen gehen sie mit uns schwimmen.	*Tomorrow they are going swimming with us.*

jagen *to hunt*	Morgen gehen sie mit uns jagen.
klettern *to climb*	Morgen gehen sie mit uns klettern.
wandern *to hike*	Morgen gehen sie mit uns wandern.
sonnenbaden *to sunbathe*	Morgen gehen sie mit uns sonnenbaden.
fischen *to fish*	Morgen gehen sie mit uns fischen.
radfahren *to bike*	Morgen gehen sie mit uns radfahren.
skilaufen *to ski*	Morgen gehen sie mit uns skilaufen.
joggen *to jog*	Morgen gehen sie mit uns joggen.
surfen *to surf*	Morgen gehen sie mit uns surfen.
einkaufen *to shop*	Morgen gehen sie mit uns einkaufen.

Using Superlatives

Superlatives describe the highest level of the meaning of an adjective or adverb. In German, superlatives most often occur in a prepositional phrase introduced by **am** (the contraction of **an** + **dem**). The suffix **-sten** is then added to the adjective or adverb. For example:

Positive Form	**Superlative Form**	
klein	am kleinsten	*smallest*
leicht	am leichtesten	*lightest, easiest*
schön	am schönsten	*prettiest, nicest*
schnell	am schnellsten	*fastest*
schwer	am schwersten	*heaviest, hardest*

If an adjective or adverb has an umlaut vowel, there is a tendency to add an umlaut to its superlative form: **jung—am jüngsten** (youngest), **alt—am ältesten** (oldest). If the adjective or adverb ends in **t**, **d**, **s**, **ss**, **ß**, **sch**, or **z**, an **-e-** is placed between the adjective and the suffix: **leicht** → **am leichtesten**. And, like in English, there are a few irregular superlative forms:

Positive Form	**Superlative Form**	
bald	am ehesten	*soonest*
groß	am größten	*biggest*
gut	am besten	*best*
hoch	am höchsten	*highest*
nah	am nächsten	*nearest*

The superlative expression with **am** is used as an adverb or predicate adjective in a sentence. For example:

Meine Tochter singt am besten. — *My daughter sings best.*

Sein Wagen ist am teuersten. — *His car is the most expensive.*

Oral Practice 10-3

 TRACK 5

Listen to the sentences on your CD. After each sentence, press "pause" and repeat it out loud. Then restate the sentence according to the following example, changing the predicate adjective to the superlative. Cover the correct answers shown on the right. Use them to compare with your own answers. Then listen to the correct answer on your CD, making sure to repeat what you hear. For example:

Meine Schwester ist schön. — *My sister is pretty.*
You say: Aber meine Schwester ist am schönsten. — *But my sister is the prettiest.*

Mein Vater ist alt. *My father is old.* — Aber mein Vater ist am ältesten.

Meine Tante is nett. *My aunt is nice.* — Aber meine Tante ist am nettesten.

Mein Fahrrad ist neu. *My bike is new.* — Aber mein Fahrrad ist am neuesten.

Mein Haus ist klein. *My house is small.* — Aber mein Haus ist am kleinsten.

Meine Familie ist groß. *My family is big.* — Aber meine Familie ist am größten.

Meine Tochter ist klug. *My daughter is smart.* — Aber meine Tochter ist am klügsten.

Meine Freundin ist jung. *My girlfriend is young.*	Aber meine Freundin ist am jüngsten.
Mein Wagen ist billig. *My car is cheap.*	Aber mein Wagen ist am billigsten.
Meine Hütte ist nah. *My cabin is near.*	Aber meine Hütte ist am nächsten.
Meine Arbeit ist gut. *My work is good.*	Aber meine Arbeit ist am besten.

GRAMMAR DEMYSTIFIED

Word Order

When an element other than the subject begins a sentence, the verb precedes the subject. Compare these sentences:

Subject Begins Sentence	Other Element Begins Sentence
Onkel Karl wohnt in den Bergen.	In den Bergen wohnt Onkel Karl.
Wir fahren morgen in die Stadt.	Morgen fahren wir in die Stadt.

Written Practice 10-1

Say each question out loud. Then give the logical answer to the question using one of the four responses provided. For example:

Wo kann man fischen gehen? Am Strand.

In der Stadt. *In the city.*	Im Wald. *In the woods.*
Am Strand. *At the beach.*	In den Bergen. *In the mountains.*

1. Wo kann man skilaufen? ______________________.
2. Wo kann man schwimmen? ______________________.
3. Wo kann man wandern? ______________________.
4. Wo kann man einkaufen gehen? ______________________.
5. Wo kann man radfahren? ______________________.
6. Wo kann man klettern? ______________________.
7. Wo kann man surfen? ______________________.

8. Wo kann man sonnenbaden? ______________________________ .
9. Wo kann man joggen? ______________________________ .
10. Wo kann man jagen gehen? ______________________________ .

VOCABULARY DEMYSTIFIED

Die vier Jahreszeiten The Four Seasons

The names of the seasons in German are **der Sommer** (*summer*), **der Herbst** (*autumn*), **der Winter** (*winter*), and **der Frühling** or **das Frühjahr** (*spring*). To say *in* a particular season, use the preposition **im** (the contraction of **in** + **dem**): **im Sommer**, **im Herbst**, **im Winter**, **im Frühling**.

Oral Practice 10-4

TRACK 6

Listen to the sentences on your CD. After each sentence press "pause" and repeat it out loud. Then restate the sentence with the appropriate season of the year. Listen to the correct answer on your CD, making sure to repeat what you hear. For example:

Es ist sehr kalt.
You say: Im Winter ist es sehr kalt. *In winter it is very cold.*

Es ist sehr heiß.

Es schneit.

Es ist regnerisch.

Es ist am kältesten.

Es ist sehr kühl.

Man kann schwimmen gehen.

Man kann skilaufen gehen.

Es ist am heißesten.

Es regnet.

Es ist schön.

Written Practice 10-2

Fill in each blank with the superlative form of the adjective or adverb shown in parentheses.

1. Mein Wagen ist ______________ . (billig)
2. Seine Großmutter ist ______________ . (alt)
3. Ist Ihr Haus ______________ ? (groß)
4. Meine Schwester ist ______________ . (klein)
5. Unsere Kinder singen ______________ . (gut)

CULTURE DEMYSTIFIED

Shaking Hands

It is very common in all parts of the German-speaking world to shake hands when greeting someone. Even if there are several people to greet, it is customary to go up to each person and shake hands when saying hello. At a party, shake hands with the host and hostess first, and then greet the other guests as well as the children. If you're not sure what is appropriate at a specific event, watch your host or others in the group and conform to what they are doing. Some useful phrases are:

Ich möchte Herrn Schmidt vorstellen.	*I would like to introduce Mr. Schmidt.*
Kennen Sie Frau Müller?	*Do you know Ms. Müller?*
Sie haben einander die Hand gegeben.	*They shook hands.*
Sabine schüttelt Herrn Keller die Hand.	*Sabine shakes Mr. Keller's hand.*
Ich möchte die neue Studentin kennen lernen.	*I would like to meet the new student.*
Sehr angenehm.	*Pleased to meet you.*

PHRASES FOR SURVIVAL

Days and Months

Add these useful words and phrases to your language arsenal to help you get by in the German-speaking world:

Die Wochentage ***Days of the Week***	**Die Monate** ***Months***
Sonntag *Sunday*	Januar *January*
Montag *Monday*	Februar *February*
Dienstag *Tuesday*	März *March*
Mittwoch *Wednesday*	April *April*
Donnerstag *Thursday*	Mai *May*
Freitag *Friday*	Juni *June*
Sonnabend/Samstag *Saturday*	Juli *July*
	August *August*
	September *September*
	Oktober *October*
	November *November*
	Dezember *December*

Handy Phrases

Heute ist Montag.	*Today is Monday.*
Wir reisen am Freitag ab.	*We depart on Friday.*
Im Januar ist es kälter als im Juni.	*It is colder in January than in June.*
Sein Geburtstag ist im März.	*His birthday is in March.*

Written Practice 10-3

The following lines of dialogue are out of sequence. Place a number, from 1 to 8, in each blank to show the appropriate order for the lines.

_____ Wie ist das Wetter?

_____ Er will nicht aufstehen. Er ist sehr müde.

_____ Ja, der Zug ist zu teuer.

______ Nicht gut. Es regnet, und es ist sehr windig.

______ Erik! Steh auf bitte!

______ Fahren wir mit der Straßenbahn zum Strand?

______ Das ist schade, aber wir fahren heute zum Strand. Ruf ihn wieder!

______ Schläft Erik noch? Es ist schon sieben Uhr.

QUIZ

Responding to questions. Listen to your CD to hear each question. Press "pause" to repeat the question out loud and select your answer—a, b, or c. Then listen to the correct answer on the CD, making sure to repeat what you hear.

1. (a) Wir gehen morgen radfahren.
   (b) Es regnet wieder.
   (c) Er schläft noch.

2. (a) Nein, mit dem Zug.
   (b) Ja, ich habe schon angerufen.
   (c) Nein, ich kann nicht aufstehen.

3. (a) Nein, im Sommer ist es heiß.
   (b) Im Winter kann man nicht schwimmen gehen.
   (c) Ja, und es ist sehr kalt.

4. (a) In der Stadt.
   (b) Im März.
   (c) Im Wald.

5. (a) Skilaufen.
   (b) Einkaufen.
   (c) Sonnenbaden.

Using each pair of words provided as your cues, say that in the month shown, the weather is the adjective shown. Listen to the correct answers on your CD, making sure to repeat what you hear. For example:

January, cold
You say: Im Januar ist es kalt. *It is cold in January.*

6. *July, hot*
7. *October, windy*
8. *April, rainy*
9. *November, cool*
10. *May, foggy*

PART TWO TEST

TRACK 8

Responding to questions. Listen to your CD to hear each question. Press "pause" to repeat the question out loud and select your answer—a, b, or c. Then listen to the correct answer on the CD, making sure to repeat what you hear.

1. (a) Er geht zur Schule.
   (b) Er ist krank.
   (c) Er trinkt lieber Milch.

2. (a) Ja, sie hat mich gern.
   (b) Nein, er ist nicht alt.
   (c) Ja, er hat sie gern.

3. (a) Ich weiß nicht. Ich sehe es nicht.
   (b) Ich glaube, du sollst den Arzt anrufen.
   (c) Ja, ich habe ihn gern.

4. (a) Nein, ich esse gern Brot mit Butter.
   (b) Ja, ich trinke lieber Mineralwasser.
   (c) Ja, ich habe Hunger.

5. (a) Kaffee.
   (b) Hähnchen.
   (c) Pilze.

6. (a) Nach Hause.
   (b) Ein Glas Rotwein.
   (c) Im Restaurant.

7. (a) Es ist vierzehn Uhr.
   (b) Fünfzig Euro.
   (c) Das ist teuer.

8. (a) Ein grünes Kleid.
   (b) Dunkelblau.
   (c) Unser neuer VW.

9. (a) Sie haben Sandalen aus Italien.
   (b) Sie trägt schwarze Stiefel.
   (c) Er trägt ein weißes Sweatshirt.

10. (a) Es ist halb zehn.
    (b) Da ist der Schalter.
    (c) Hast du die Fahrkarten?

11. (a) Ja, ich muss in der Stadt bleiben.
    (b) Nein, sprechen Sie bitte Englisch!
    (c) Ja, wir gehen zum Restaurant.

12. (a) Ja, sie sind jung.
    (b) Nein, sein Bruder ist älter.
    (c) Ja, das ist viel besser.

13. (a) Wir gehen morgen skilaufen.
    (b) Es regnet wieder.
    (c) Im März ist es noch kühl.

14. (a) Nein, im Sommer ist es heiß.
    (b) Im Winter kann man nicht schwimmen gehen.
    (c) Im Frühling ist schönes Wetter.

15. (a) In der Stadt.
    (b) Am Dienstag.
    (c) Am Strand.

Using the word or phrase provided as your cue, say that *Erik sees* that person or object. Listen to the correct answers on your CD, making sure to repeat what you hear. For example:

female teacher
You say: Erik sieht die Lehrerin.

16. *museum*
17. *train station*
18. *doctor*
19. *bridge*
20. *boots*

Using the words provided as your cues, say *I do not eat* the food or *I do not drink* the beverage indicated. Listen to the correct answers on your CD, making sure to repeat what you hear. For example:

bread
You say: Ich esse kein Brot.

21. *milk*
22. *tea*
23. *fruit*
24. *eggs*
25. *coffee*

PART THREE

DAILY LIFE

CHAPTER 11

Rich and Poor

In this chapter you will learn:

Buying das Geschenk *(the Gift)*

Showing Possession with the Genitive Case

Using the Phrase Was für (ein) ... *?*

Buying *das Geschenk* (the Gift)

 TRACK 9

Listen to the following dialogue on your CD. After you hear a phrase or sentence on a track, always press "pause" and repeat what you hear.

CHRISTIAN: Rat mal, was Andrea ihrem Verlobten schenkt! — *Guess what Andrea is giving her fiancé!*

BRITTA: Ich weiß es. Sie kauft ihm eine Armbanduhr, eine aus Gold. — *I know. She is buying him a watch, a gold one.*

CHRISTIAN: Wie teuer das ist! Aber Andrea ist sehr großzügig und liebt Ralf sehr. — *That is so expensive! But Andrea is very generous and loves Ralf very much.*

BRITTA: Und ihr Vater ist reich. Er hat ihr ein neues Kabrio geschenkt. — *And her father is rich. He bought her a new convertible.*

CHRISTIAN: Sie hat Glück, dass sie nicht arbeiten muss. — *She is lucky she does not have to work.*

BRITTA: Das ist wahr. Aber sie hat nicht immer genug Geld. Ich musste ihr vorgestern zwanzig Euro leihen. — *That is true. But she does not always have enough money. The day before yesterday, I had to lend her twenty euros.*

CHRISTIAN: Sie ist manchmal ein bisschen leichtsinnig. — *Sometimes she is a little irresponsible.*

BRITTA: Und trotzdem ein sehr sympathisches Mädchen. — *And despite that a very likable girl.*

Dialogue Review

Answer the following questions about the dialogue Buying **das Geschenk**. Cover the correct answers shown on the right. Use them to compare with your own answers.

1. Was kauft Andrea ihrem Verlobten? — Sie kauft ihrem Verlobten eine Armbanduhr.

   What is Andrea buying for her fiancé?

2. Wer ist reich? — Andreas Vater ist reich.

   Who is rich?

3. Warum hat Andrea Glück? — Sie muss nicht arbeiten.
   Why is Andrea lucky?

4. Was musste Britta Andrea leihen? — Sie musste Andrea zwanzig Euro leihen.
   What did Britta have to lend to Andrea?

5. Wer ist leichtsinnig? — Andrea ist leichtsinnig.
   Who is irresponsible?

SHOWING POSSESSION WITH THE GENITIVE CASE

Many German possessives are formed in the same way as in English: an **-s** is added to the word, which indicates possession. However, German does not require the use of an apostrophe when forming a possessive. This type of possessive construction is used with names.

Andreas Geschenk ist teuer.	*Andrea's gift is expensive.*
Christians Mutter ist krank.	*Christian's mother is sick.*

To show possession with other nouns in German, the *genitive case* must be used. With masculine and neuter nouns in the genitive, both the article or other modifier and the noun will have an **-(e)s** ending.

des Mannes	*of the man/the man's*
dieses Bahnhofs	*of this train station/this train station's*
eines Kindes	*of a child/a child's*
meines Flugzeugs	*of my airplane/my airplane's*

Note: *An* **-es** *ending is generally used to make a monosyllabic word easier to pronounce.*

Feminine and neuter nouns in the genitive require an **-er** ending on the article or modifier but none on the noun.

der Frau	*of the woman/the woman's*
einer Lehrerin	*of a teacher/a teacher's*

deiner Sandalen	*of your sandals/your sandals'*
dieser Grenzen	*of these borders/these borders'*

Written Practice 11-1

Using each pair of words provided as your cues, form a *possessive* with the first person indicated and say that *the second person is generous*. For example:

Karl, Vater   Karls Vater ist großzügig.

1. Britta, Mutter ______________________.
2. Tina, Onkel ______________________.
3. Werner, Bruder ______________________.
4. Andrea, Schwester ______________________.
5. Ralf, Freundin ______________________.
6. Gabi, Verlobter ______________________.
7. Stefan, Arzt ______________________.
8. Angela, Kinder ______________________.
9. Christoph, Tochter ______________________.
10. Sonja, Eltern ______________________.

Oral Practice 11-1

TRACK 10

Listen to your CD to hear questions that ask *whose* (**wessen**) friend or relative is *finally well*. Press "pause" to repeat each question. Then answer the question using the noun in parentheses, forming it in the genitive case. Listen to the correct answer, making sure to repeat what you hear. For example:

Wessen Vater ist endlich gesund? (der Professor)
You say: Der Vater des Professors ist endlich gesund.   *The professor's father is finally well.*

Wessen Bruder ist endlich gesund? (der Lehrer)

Wessen Tante ist endlich gesund? (der Arzt)

Wessen Mutter ist endlich gesund? (das Kind)

Wessen Freund ist endlich gesund? (das Mädchen)

Wessen Eltern sind endlich gesund? (der Schaffner)

Wessen Kinder sind endlich gesund? (der Kellner)

Wessen Freundin ist endlich gesund? (mein Bruder)

Wessen Tochter ist endlich gesund? (dein Freund)

Follow the previous directions, but now say that the person's friend or relative is very tired. For example:

> Wessen Vater ist sehr müde? (die Lehrerin)
> *You say*: Der Vater der Lehrerin ist sehr müde. *The teacher's father is very tired.*

Wessen Mutter ist sehr müde? (deine Tante)

Wessen Sohn ist sehr müde? (deine Freundin)

Wessen Kind ist sehr müde? (meine Professorin)

Wessen Bruder ist sehr müde? (meine Frau)

Wessen Eltern sind sehr müde? (diese Kinder)

Wessen Professor ist sehr müde? (diese Studentin)

Wessen Kinder sind sehr müde? (diese Touristin)

Oral Practice 11-2

TRACK 11

Listen to your CD to hear a series of statements. Press "pause" to repeat each one. Then restate the sentence with the phrase **Ich weiß, dass ...** (I know that . . .). Listen to the correct answer, making sure to repeat what you hear. For example:

> Dein Vater ist wieder krank.
> *You say*: Ich weiß, dass dein Vater wieder krank ist. *I know that your father father is sick again.*

Martin wohnt in Hamburg.

Tina ist leichtsinnig.

Berlin ist größer als Bonn.

Der Zug kommt um zwei Uhr.

GRAMMAR DEMYSTIFIED

Conjunctions

With the conjunctions **und** (*and*), **aber** (*but*), **oder** (*or*), and **denn** (*because*), the common word order in a German sentence is not changed when two sentences are joined by the conjunction. In both sentences, the subject will precede the verb. For example:

Karl ist reich, und Tina ist arm.	*Karl is rich, and Tina is poor.*
Er isst Kompott aber möchte lieber Eis.	*He eats stewed fruit but prefers ice cream.*
Wir gehen ins Kino oder gehen einkaufen.	*We are going to the movies or going shopping.*
Gabi schläft noch, denn sie ist müde.	*Gabi is still sleeping, because she is tired.*

Note: *Just as in English, the German subject of the second sentence is often understood and not stated.*

When using all other conjunctions, such as **dass** (*that*) and **weil** (*because*), the conjugated verb becomes the final element in the sentence. For example:

Ich weiß, dass Angela kein Geld <u>hat</u>.	*I know that Angela has no money.*
Gabi schläft noch, weil sie müde <u>ist</u>.	*Gabi is still sleeping because she is tired.*

Die Kinder spielen Fußball.

Du hast genug Geld.

Ihr könnt es nicht verstehen.

Er ist in der Stadt gewesen.

Follow the previous directions, but now use the introductory phrase **Er ist zu Hause, weil ...** (He is at home, because . . .).

Er ist sehr krank.

Das Wetter ist schlecht.

Es regnet.

Es hat geschneit.

Er muss lernen.

Er kann nicht aufstehen.

Er liest ein gutes Buch.

Using the Phrase *Was für (ein) ... ?*

The expression **Was für (ein) ... ?** comes in handy when asking what something is like in German. If the noun in question is plural, omit **ein** from the phrase, but whether singular or plural nouns are involved, the meaning of the phrase is the same: *What kind of . . . ?* For example:

Singular Nouns

was für ein Mann	*what kind of man*
was für eine Lehrerin	*what kind of teacher*
was für eine Speisekarte	*what kind of menu*
was für ein Bett	*what kind of bed*

Plural Nouns

was für Bücher	*what kind of books*
was für Schuhe	*what kind of shoes*
was für Kinder	*what kind of children*
was für Autos	*what kind of automobiles*

Note: *The phrase* **was für** *(without* **ein***) is also used with singular collectives:* **Geld**, **Brot**, **Eis**, *and so on.*

Oral Practice 11-3

TRACK 12

Using the pairs of nouns and adjectives provided as your cues, ask *what kind of* the noun. Then respond to the question using the adjective provided. Listen to your CD to hear the correct questions and responses, making sure to repeat what you hear. For example:

Buch, altes
You say: Was für ein Buch ist das? Das ist ein altes Buch.

Auto, neues

Schule, gute

Schuhe, braune

Bahnhof, größer

Kinder, nette

Geld, amerikanisches

Autos, deutsche

Mädchen, schönes

Follow the previous directions, however, this time using a different type of sentence. Be sure to respond to each question appropriately, and then listen to the correct questions and responses on your CD, making sure to repeat what you hear. For example:

Buch, altes
You say: Was für ein Buch haben Sie? Ich habe ein altes Buch.

Haus, kleines

Handschuhe, warme

Zeitung, englische

Wagen, roten

Stiefel, schwarze

Koffer, schweren

Armbanduhr, neue

GRAMMAR DEMYSTIFIED

Indirect Objects

If a noun is used as an *indirect object* that noun must be in the dative case. (To identify the indirect object in a sentence, ask *to whom* or *for whom* of the verb.) Masculine and neuter nouns add the ending **-em** to articles and other modifiers in the dative case.

Masculine

Ich gebe dem Mann € 2,00.	*I give the man 2 euros.*
Ich sende meinem Bruder einen Brief.	*I send my brother a letter.*

Neuter

Ich schenke dem Kind € 5,00.	*I give the child 5 euros.*
Ich gebe diesem Mädchen ein Geschenk.	*I give this girl a gift.*

Feminine nouns add the ending **-er** in the dative case.

Er gibt der Frau € 10,00.	*He gives the woman 10 euros.*
Er schenkt deiner Mutter eine Rose.	*He gives your mother a rose.*

And plural nouns add the ending **-en** to the articles and other modifiers. In addition, if the plural noun itself does not end in **-n**, an **-n** is added.

Ich gebe den Kindern ein Geschenk.	*I give the children a gift.*
Er schenkt deinen Eltern ein Buch.	*He gives your parents a book.*

Also, note that if the indirect object in a sentence is a pronoun, its dative case form must be used.

Nominative	Dative	Nominative	Dative
ich	mir	wir	uns
du	dir	ihr	euch
er	ihm	Sie	Ihnen
sie	ihr	sie	ihnen
es	ihm		

For example:

Wir geben ihm ein neues Hemd.	*We give him a new shirt.*

CULTURE DEMYSTIFIED

The Euro

Many countries in Europe now use the same currency—the euro. Because there are various languages involved with this currency, prices are not always written with words but rather with numbers. And the word *euro* is symbolized by **€**. So, prices will look like this:

€ 10,50	*or*	10,50 €
€ 205,75	*or*	205,75 €

Notice in these numbers that a comma is used where in English a decimal point would be used.

Oral Practice 11-4

TRACK 13

Listen to your CD to hear a series of questions that ask *to whom* (**wem**) something is being given. Press "pause" to repeat each question. Then answer the question with the words in parentheses. Listen to the correct answer, making sure to repeat what you hear. For example:

Wem gibt er das Buch? (der Lehrer)
You say: Er gibt dem Lehrer das Buch. *He gives the teacher the book.*

Wem gibt er das Geld? (die Lehrerin)

Wem gibt er die Rose? (seine Freundin)

Wem schenkt er die CD? (sein Freund)

Wem schenkt er das Hemd? (sein Vater)

Wem gibst du die Bluse? (meine Mutter)

Wem gibst du das Geschenk? (die Kinder)

Wem schenkst du die Handschuhe? (unser Onkel)

Wem schenkst du die Ohrringe? (unsere Tante)

Wem sendet sie den Brief? (ihre Eltern)

Wem sendet sie das Geld? (ihr Professor)

Written Practice 11-2

Fill in each blank with the dative form of the word or words in parentheses.

1. Was geben Sie _______________ ? (der Mann)
2. Ich schenke _______________ ein Hemd. (du)
3. Er hat _______________ eine Rose gegeben. (seine Schwester)
4. Wir werden _______________ einen Brief senden. (Sie)
5. Ich will _______________ ein Buch schenken. (die Kinder)

PHRASES FOR SURVIVAL

Signage

Add these useful words and phrases to your language arsenal to help you get by in the German-speaking world:

Eingang	*entrance*
Kein Eingang	*not an entrance*
Ausgang	*exit*
Kein Ausgang	*not an exit*
Kasse	*checkout, cashier*
Fahrstuhl	*elevator*
Treppe	*stairway*
Rauchen verboten	*no smoking*

Written Practice 11-3

The following lines of dialogue are out of sequence. Place a number, from 1 to 8, in each blank to show the appropriate order for the lines.

_____ Das ist wahr. Aber er ist nicht arm und hat immer genug Geld.

_____ Wie teuer das ist! Aber Dirk ist sehr reich.

_____ Nein, sein Vater ist reich. Nicht Dirk.

_____ Ja, er kauft ihr Ohrringe, aus Gold.

_____ Und wie! Gestern hat er mir dreißig Euro geliehen.

_____ Er ist auch ein sehr sympathischer und guter Freund.

_____ Weißt du, was Dirk seiner Verlobten schenkt?

_____ Und Dirk ist sehr großzügig.

QUIZ

Responding to questions. Listen to your CD to hear each question. Press "pause" to repeat the question out loud and select your answer—a, b, or c. Then listen to the correct answer on the CD, making sure to repeat what you hear.

1. (a) Der Bruder meiner Freundin.
   (b) Das Kind seines Sohnes.
   (c) Sabines Sohn.

2. (a) Die Tochter meines Bruders schläft noch.
   (b) Sie schenkt ihm eine Armbanduhr.
   (c) Er ist nicht müde und arbeitet noch.

3. (a) Eines Freundes.
   (b) Einem Freund.
   (c) Ein Freund.

4. (a) Sie möchte einen roten Pulli.
   (b) Der Vater dieses Mädchens möchte einen weißen Pulli.
   (c) Ich möchte einen dunkelblauen Pulli.

5. (a) Sie geben uns das Geld.
   (b) Nein, sie haben kein Geld.
   (c) Herr Keller gibt ihm das Geld.

Using each pair of words provided as your cues, say that you give *the object* shown to *the person* shown. Listen to the correct answers on your CD, making sure to repeat what you hear. For example:

mein Vater, das Geld
You say: Ich gebe meinem Vater das Geld. *I give my father the money.*

6. Werner, der Brief
7. deine Frau, eine Rose
8. die Kinder, ein Buch
9. du, ein Geschenk
10. der Professor, die Handschuhe

CHAPTER 12

Car Trouble

In this chapter you will learn:

Making die Reparatur *(Repairs)*

Asking Who, Whom, and Whose

Making *die Reparatur* (Repairs)

TRACK 15

Listen to the following dialogue on your CD. After you hear a phrase or sentence on a track, always press "pause" and repeat what you hear.

HERR BENZ: Die Windschutzscheibe ist gesprungen. Eine Neue muss vom Hersteller bestellt werden.	*The windshield is cracked. A new one has to be ordered from the manufacturer.*

FRAU MANN: Wie lange wird es dauern die Neue zu bekommen? — *How long will it take to get the new one?*

HERR BENZ: Nur einen Tag. Und diese Reparatur verlangt nur zwei Stunden. — *Only one day. And this repair takes only two hours.*

FRAU MANN: Aber ich muss heute abend in Darmstadt sein. — *But I have to be in Darmstadt this evening.*

HERR BENZ: Vielleicht wollen Sie einen Wagen mieten. Wir vermieten sie. — *Perhaps you want to rent a car. We lease them.*

FRAU MANN: Gute Idee! Ich brauche einen größeren Wagen für fünf Personen. — *Good idea. I need a rather big car for five people.*

HERR BENZ: Schön! Die Gebühr für zwei Tage und die Versicherung betragen achtzig Euro. — *Fine! The fee for two days and the insurance comes to eighty euros.*

FRAU MANN: Nehmen Sie Reiseschecks an? — *Do you accept traveler's checks?*

HERR BENZ: Selbstverständlich. — *Of course.*

Dialogue Review

Answer the following questions about the dialogue Making **die Reparatur**. Cover the correct answers shown on the right. Use them to compare with your own answers.

1. Was ist gesprungen?
   What is cracked?
   Die Windschutzscheibe ist gesprungen.

2. Wie lange dauert diese Reparatur?
   How long does this repair take?
   Diese Reparatur dauert nur zwei Stunden.

3. Wo muss Frau Mann heute abend sein?
   Where does Ms. Mann have to be this evening?
   Sie muss heute abend in Darmstadt sein.

4. Was vermietet Herr Benz? — Er vermietet Wagen.
   What does Mr. Benz rent?

5. Nimmt Herr Benz Reiseschecks an? — Ja, er nimmt Reiseschecks an.
   Does Mr. Benz accept traveler's checks?

The verb **betragen** (*to come to, to amount to*) is used with singular or plural subjects to identify sums of money or collectives such as *time*. For example:

Die Gebühr beträgt fünf Euro.	*The fee comes to five euros.*
Ihre Einkäufe betragen zehn Euro.	*Your purchases come to ten euros.*
Die Zeitdifferenz zwischen Berlin und Washington, DC, beträgt sechs Stunden.	*The time difference between Berlin and Washington, DC, comes to six hours.*

GRAMMAR DEMYSTIFIED

Accusative Prepositions

Chapter 6 discussed how German direct objects are expressed in the accusative case: **Ich sehe <u>den Bahnhof</u>.** That same case is used after certain prepositions, among them **durch** (through), **für** (for), **ohne** (without), and **um** (around). Consider these example sentences:

Der Zug fährt durch einen Tunnel.	*The train goes through a tunnel.*
Er arbeitet für seine Tante.	*He works for his aunt.*
Sie kommt ohne ihren Mann.	*She comes without her husband.*
Das Kino ist hier um die Ecke.	*The movie theater is here around the corner.*

If a pronoun follows one of these prepositions, the pronoun must also be in the accusative case: **Ich habe ein Geschenk <u>für ihn</u>.** (*I have a gift for him.*)

Written Practice 12-1

Respond to each question asking for whom this invitation is intended, putting the noun or pronoun in parentheses in the accusative case. For example:

Ist diese Einladung für den Lehrer? (er)	Nein, diese Einladung ist für ihn. *No, this invitation is for him.*

1. Ist diese Einladung für deinen Freund? (sie) ________________.
2. Ist diese Einladung für deine Freundin? (du) ________________.
3. Ist diese Einladung für meine Mutter? (Sie) ________________.
4. Ist diese Einladung für deinen Onkel? (mein Professor) ________________.
5. Ist diese Einladung für den Arzt? (die Ärztin) ________________.
6. Ist diese Einladung für ihn? (wir) ________________.
7. Ist diese Einladung für Martin? (ihr) ________________.
8. Ist diese Einladung für Frau Mann? (ich) ________________.
9. Ist diese Einladung für dich? (meine Cousine) ________________.
10. Ist diese Einladung für deine Schwester? (mein Bruder) ________________.

Oral Practice 12-1

Use the nouns provided to tell what place we went through. Cover the correct answers shown on the right. Use them to compare with your own answers. Then listen to the correct answers on your CD, making sure to repeat what you hear. For example:

das Haus	*house*
You say: Wir sind durch das Haus gegangen.	*We went through the house.*

das Dorf *village*	Wir sind durch das Dorf gegangen.
der Bahnhof *train station*	Wir sind durch den Bahnhof gegangen.
die Schule *school*	Wir sind durch die Schule gegangen.
die Stadt *city*	Wir sind durch die Stadt gegangen.

der Hafen *harbor* Wir sind durch den Hafen gegangen.

der Wald *woods* Wir sind durch den Wald gegangen.

Follow the previous directions; however, this time ask a question. For example:

das Hotel *hotel*
You say: Fahren Sie um das Hotel? *Are you driving around the hotel?*

die Kirche *church* Fahren Sie um die Kirche?

der See *lake* Fahren Sie um den See?

das Rathaus *townhall* Fahren Sie um das Rathaus?

der Platz *square* Fahren Sie um den Platz?

der Park *park* Fahren Sie um den Park?

das Krankenhaus *hospital* Fahren Sie um das Krankenhaus?

Using the same directions, follow the example.

sein Bruder *his brother*
You say: Er spielt nicht ohne seinen Bruder. *He won't play without his brother.*

sein Freund *his friend* Er spielt nicht ohne seinen Freund.

der Mechaniker *mechanic* Er spielt nicht ohne den Mechaniker.

unser Chef *our boss* Er spielt nicht ohne unseren Chef.

ich *I* Er spielt nicht ohne mich.

du *you* Er spielt nicht ohne dich.

wir *we* Er spielt nicht ohne uns.

VOCABULARY DEMYSTIFIED

Car Care

As in many places, there are gas stations (**Tankstellen**) in Germany that offer *self-service*. If that's what you prefer, watch for the word **Selbstbedienung** or the abbreviation **SB**. Most of these stations offer only gas (**Benzin**). If major repairs are needed, find a specialized garage (**Reparaturwerkstatt**).

GRAMMAR DEMYSTIFIED

Translating Prepositions

Sometimes English and German use similar expressions, and direct translations can easily be made. However, there are many instances when a direct translation between these languages cannot be made. Three such cases are with the use of the prepositions in the expressions **warten auf** (*to wait for*), **reden über** (*to talk about*), and **denken an** (*to think about*). Practice saying the following questions and answers that use these three useful expressions:

Auf wen wartet Herr Benz?	Herr Benz wartet auf seine Frau.
Auf wen warten Sie?	Ich warte auf einen Freund.
Auf wen wartet deine Cousine?	Meine Cousine wartet auf mich.
Über wen reden sie?	Sie reden über Frau Mann.
Über wen reden die Mädchen?	Die Mädchen reden über Werner.
Über wen redest du?	Ich rede über meinen Verlobten.
An wen denkst du?	Ich denke an meine Eltern.
An wen denkt Herr Schneider?	Herr Schneider denkt an seinen Bruder.
An wen denkt sie?	Sie denkt an den Mechaniker.

Asking Who, Whom, and Whose

In informal style, English doesn't always distinguish between the subjective case *who* and the objective case *whom*, preferring to use *who* in both instances. But German always makes that distinction. For example:

Nominative	Accusative	Dative	Possessive
wer	wen	wem	wessen

To ask about the subject of a sentence, use **wer**:

Wer wohnt in diesem Haus?	*Who lives in this house?*

To ask about the direct object of a sentence or about the word that follows an accusative preposition, use **wen**:

Wen hast du in Berlin besucht?	*Who(m) did you visit in Berlin?*
Für wen arbeitet dein Vater?	*Who(m) does your father work for?*

To ask about the indirect object of a sentence, use **wem**:

Wem schenken Sie diese Bücher?	*Who(m) are you giving these books to?*

And to ask who possesses something, use **wessen**:

Wessen Reiseschecks sind das?	*Whose traveler's checks are those?*

Oral Practice 12-2

TRACK 17

Listen to your CD to hear the sentences. Press "pause" to repeat each one. Then, using the underlined word or phrase as your cue, ask a question with **wer**, **wen**, **wem**, or **wessen**, appropriately. Listen to the correct answer, making sure to repeat what you hear. For example:

Der Lehrer ist sehr jung.
You say: Wer ist sehr jung?

Meine Mutter hat die Reiseschecks.

Ich gebe Ihnen fünf Euro.

Wir haben unseren Onkel besucht.

Dieses Geschenk ist für ihn.

Sein Vater hat keine Versicherung.

Erik sendet mir ein Telegramm.

Tina kommt ohne ihre Cousine.

Er lernt den Mechaniker kennen.

Der Bruder meines Freundes ist krank.

Sie hat es für ihre Tochter gekauft.

GRAMMAR DEMYSTIFIED

Dative Prepositions

Chapter 11 addressed indirect objects, which require the dative case in German. Just as there are accusative prepositions, there are also prepositions that require the dative case. Some of these are **aus** (*out*), **bei** (*at*, *by*), **mit** (*with*), **von** (*from*, *of*), and **zu** (*to*). Consider these example sentences:

Warum trinkst du aus der Flasche?	*Why are you drinking out of the bottle?*
Karl wohnt bei seinen Freunden.	*Karl lives at his friends' house.*
Ich spreche mit dem Polizisten.	*I speak with the police officer.*
Das ist ein Geschenk von meiner Freundin.	*That is a gift from my girlfriend.*
Die Kinder laufen zum Park.	*The children run to the park.*

If a pronoun follows a dative preposition, the pronoun's dative form must be used: **Mit wem sprichst du? Ich spreche mit ihr.** (Who[m] are you speaking with? I am speaking with her.)

> **NOTE:** *To say* at *or* to someone's house, *German uses the prepositions* **bei** *and* **zu** *but omits the word* **Haus**, *whereas in English the word* house *is often included:* **bei meiner Freundin/zu meiner Freundin** = at my girlfriend's house/to my girlfriend's house.

Oral Practice 12-3

TRACK 18

Listen to your CD to hear questions that contain dative prepositions. Press "pause" to repeat each question. Then, using the word or phrase in parentheses as your cue, answer the question appropriately. Listen to the correct answer, making sure to repeat what you hear. For example:

> Mit wem spricht sie? (der Lehrer)
> *You say*: Sie spricht mit dem Lehrer.

Mit wem spielt er? (sein Bruder)

Von wem hast du den Brief bekommen? (mein Freund)

Bei wem wohnen sie? (ihre Eltern)

Zu wem geht sie heute abend? (ihre Tante)

Mit wem reden Sie? (er)

Von wem sind die Rosen? (ich)

Bei wem schläfst du morgen? (meine Großeltern)

Zu wem fährt sie? (wir)

Using the same directions, follow the example.

> Sprechen Sie mit Martin? (der Lehrer)
> *You say*: Nein, ich spreche mit dem Lehrer.

Kommt sie aus dem Hotel? (das Krankenhaus)

Fahren Sie jetzt zur Kirche? (das Rathaus)

Seid ihr mit dem Bus gefahren? (der Zug)

Ist das Geschenk von deinem Onkel? (meine Tante)

Kommen die Kinder aus der Schule? (die Kirche)

Wohnst du bei Frau Mann? (meine Cousine)

Ist das ein Freund von ihm? (sie)

Written Practice 12-2

Fill in each blank, choosing the appropriate preposition in parentheses.

1. Meine Mutter arbeitet ______________ eine reiche Frau. (mit/für/zu)
2. Wohnst du noch ______________ deiner Großmutter? (bei/ohne/um)
3. Das Mädchen will nicht ______________ ihren Bruder spielen. (zu/von/ohne)
4. Der alte Mann kommt ______________ dem Krankenhaus. (aus/mit/durch)
5. Ich möchte ______________ dem Chef sprechen. (um/mit/über)

PHRASES FOR SURVIVAL

Stopping at a Gas Station

Add these useful phrases to your language arsenal to help you get by in the German-speaking world:

Ich habe eine Panne.	*My car broke down./I have a flat.*
Volltanken bitte!	*Fill it up, please!*
Bitte prüfen Sie das Öl!	*Please check the oil.*
Ich habe kein Benzin mehr.	*I have run out of gas.*
Hier ist mein Führerschein.	*Here is my license.*
Wo ist die Autobahn?	*Where is the autobahn (superhighway)?*

Written Practice 12-3

The following lines of dialogue are out of sequence. Place a number, from 1 to 8, in each blank to show the appropriate order for the lines.

______ Gut. Das ist nicht zu teuer.
______ Wir vermieten Wagen. Möchten Sie einen Wagen mieten?
______ Wie lange wird die Reparatur dauern?
______ Sie brauchen eine neue Windschutzscheibe. Diese ist gesprungen.

______ Schön! Die Gebühr für drei Tage beträgt neunzig Euro.
______ Aber ich muss heute in München sein.
______ Ja, bitte! Einen kleinen Wagen für zwei Personen.
______ Vielleicht zwei Tage.

QUIZ

TRACK 19

Responding to questions. Listen to your CD to hear each question. Press "pause" to repeat the question out loud and select your answer—a, b, or c. Then listen to the correct answer on your CD, making sure to repeat what you hear.

1. (a) Er bekommt keine Einladung.
   (b) Die Einladung ist für dich.
   (c) Nein, er hat keine Einladung.

2. (a) Hier vermietet man Wagen.
   (b) Man hat einen großen Wagen gemietet.
   (c) Frau Mann muss einen Wagen mieten.

3. (a) Heute abend.
   (b) Am Freitag.
   (c) Vier Stunden.

4. (a) Der Mechaniker.
   (b) Das Krankenhaus und das Rathaus.
   (c) Der Zug nach Darmstadt.

5. (a) Ich muss mit dem Chef sprechen.
   (b) Er kann nicht sprechen.
   (c) Wir sprechen nicht mit ihr.

Using each pair of words in parentheses as your cues, say that *the first person* shown works for *the second person* shown. Listen to the correct answers on your CD, making sure to repeat what you hear. For example:

mein Vater, Frau Mann
You say: Mein Vater arbeitet für Frau Mann. *My father works for Ms. Mann.*

6. seine Eltern, der Lehrer
7. ich, sein Onkel
8. du, ihre Tante
9. Herr Benz, wir
10. meine Tochter, sie

CHAPTER 13

Taking Time for Fun

In this chapter you will learn:

Auf die Pauke hauen *Painting the Town Red*
Talking About Today, Yesterday, and Tomorrow
Simple Past Tense
Asking Specific Questions with Interrogatives

Auf die Pauke hauen Painting the Town Red

 TRACK 20

Listen to the following dialogue on your CD. After you hear a phrase or sentence on a track, always press "pause" and repeat what you hear.

HORST: Hast du Lust, heute abend ins Theater zu gehen? „Faust“ wird aufgeführt.	*Do you feel like going to the theater tonight? They are putting on* Faust.
FRANZISKA: Ich würde lieber in die Oper gehen. Es gibt „Die Fledermaus“ von Strauß.	*I would rather go to the opera. They are performing* Die Fledermaus *by Strauss.*
HORST: Ich habe gehört, dass die heutige Vorstellung schon ausverkauft ist.	*I heard that tonight's performance is sold out.*
FRANZISKA: Schade. Interessierst du dich für die moderne Kunst?	*Too bad. Are you interested in modern art?*
HORST: Natürlich. Gibt es eine neue Ausstellung in der Kunstgallerie?	*Naturally. Is there a new exhibition in the art gallery?*
FRANZISKA: Ja, Werke von Picasso und von einem neuen Künstler aus der Schweiz.	*Yes, works by Picasso and a new artist from Switzerland.*
HORST: Das geht. Aber vergiss nicht, dass der neue Tanzklub gerade neben der Gallerie ist.	*That would be all right. But do not forget that the new dance club is right next to the gallery.*
FRANZISKA: Ich kapiere. Wir gehen heute abend tanzen.	*I get it. We are going dancing tonight.*
HORST: Du kannst mich immer leicht durchschauen!	*You can always see right through me!*

Dialogue Review

Answer the following questions about the dialogue **Auf die Pauke hauen**. Cover the correct answers shown on the right. Use them to compare with your own answers.

1. Hat Franziska Lust ins Theater zu gehen? *Does Franzika feel like going to the theater?*	Nein, sie würde lieber in die Oper gehen.

2. Was ist schon ausverkauft?
   What is already sold out?

   Die heutige Vorstellung von „Die Fledermaus" ist schon ausverkauft.

3. Wer interessiert sich für die moderne Kunst?
   Who is interested in modern art?

   Horst interessiert sich für die moderne Kunst.

4. Wessen Werke kann man in der Kunstgallerie sehen?
   Whose works can be seen at the art gallery?

   Man kann Werke von Picasso und einem neuen Künstler aus der Schweiz sehen.

5. Wohin gehen Franziska und Horst heute abend?
   Where are Franziska and Horst going this evening?

   Heute abend gehen Franziska und Horst zum Tanzklub.

Talking About Today, Yesterday, and Tomorrow

When talking about different times of day in German, there is a variety of adverbial expressions that include the words **heute**, **gestern**, and **morgen**. Some are similar to English, and others have their own unique form.

heute	*today*
heute morgen	*this morning*
heute nachmittag	*this afternoon*
heute abend	*this evening*
heute nacht	*tonight*
gestern	*yesterday*
gestern morgen	*yesterday morning*
gestern abend	*yesterday evening*
gestern nacht	*last night*

morgen	*tomorrow*
morgen früh	*tomorrow morning*
morgen nachmittag	*tomorrow afternoon*
morgen abend	*tomorrow evening*
morgen nacht	*tomorrow night*

 **TRACK 21**

Listen to your CD to hear sentences that deal with adverbs of time. Press "pause" after each sentence and repeat what you hear.

Ich hatte heute eine Prüfung.	*I had a test today.*
Ich hatte heute morgen keine Zeit.	*I had no time this morning.*
Wir hatten heute abend viele Gäste.	*We had a lot of guests this evening.*
Wir hatten alle heute nacht viel Spaß.	*We all had a good time tonight.*
Horst war gestern in der Schweiz.	*Horst was in Switzerland yesterday.*
Horst war gestern morgen in Österreich.	*Horst was in Austria yesterday morning.*
Sie waren gestern abend bei Verwandten.	*They were at their relatives' house yesterday evening.*
Sie waren gestern nachmittag noch im Ausland.	*They were still abroad yesterday afternoon.*
Morgen kommt der Richter zu Besuch.	*The judge is coming for a visit tomorrow.*
Morgen früh kommt ein Schauspieler zu Besuch.	*An actor is coming for a visit tomorrow morning.*
Morgen nachmittag kommt jemand zu Besuch.	*Someone is coming for a visit tomorrow afternoon.*
Morgen abend kommt niemand zu Besuch.	*No one is coming for a visit tomorrow evening.*

Simple Past Tense

An action that takes place in the past is usually expressed in the *present perfect tense* (see Chapter 7) in spoken German. The simple past tense is used in written narratives or in spoken German when relating aspects of a story or an event.

The simple past tense requires the suffix **-te** + appropriate conjugational endings. For example:

Pronoun	**machen**	**lernen**	**arbeiten**	(*to make, to learn, to work*)
ich	machte	lernte	arbeitete	(*I made, learned, worked*)
du	machtest	lerntest	arbeitetest	(*you made, learned, worked*)
er, sie, es	machte	lernte	arbeitete	(*he/she/it made, learned, worked*)
wir	machten	lernten	arbeiteten	(*we made, learned, worked*)
ihr	machtet	lerntet	arbeitetet	(*you made, learned, worked*)
sie, Sie	machten	lernten	arbeiteten	(*they/you made, learned, worked*)

Note that if the stem of the verb ends in **-d** or **-t**, an extra **-e-** is inserted before the past tense ending is added: **arbeiten → ich arbeitete, du arbeitetest**; **reden → ich redete, du redetest**.

Numerous verbs are irregular in the past tense. Some become a completely new verb, others make a vowel change, and still others make a vowel change and add a suffix. Here are some examples:

Pronoun	**sein**	**kommen**	**bringen**	(*to be, to come, to bring*)
ich	war	kam	brachte	(*I was, came, brought*)
du	warst	kamst	brachtest	(*you were, came, brought*)
er, sie, es	war	kam	brachte	(*he/she/it was, came, brought*)
wir	waren	kamen	brachten	(*we were, came, brought*)
ihr	wart	kamt	brachtet	(*you were, came, brought*)
sie, Sie	waren	kamen	brachten	(*they/you were, came, brought*)

Check the appendix of your German dictionary or textbook for a full list of verb irregularities in the past tense.

TRACK 22

Listen to your CD to hear the following sentences pronounced. Press "pause" and repeat each one.

Jemand machte die Tür auf.	*Someone opened the door.*
Niemand machte die Fenster zu.	*No one closed the windows.*

Die alte Dame legte sich hin.	*The old woman lay down.*
Das junge Ehepaar tanzte stundenlang.	*The young couple danced for hours.*
Der letzte Flohmarkt fand am Freitag statt.	*The last flea market took place on Friday.*
Der Kunde schuldete mir noch Geld.	*The customer still owed me money.*
Sie amüsierten sich gut auf dem Fest.	*They really enjoyed themselves at the party.*
Wer veranstaltete die Ausstellung?	*Who put on the exhibition?*
Wir bekamen die Eintrittskarten.	*We received the tickets.*
Erik sprach mit der jungen Schauspielerin.	*Erik spoke with the young actress.*
Ich verstand das Stück nicht.	*I did not understand the play.*
Im Kino lief ein neuer Spielfilm.	*A new feature film ran at the movie theater.*
In der Diskothek war nicht viel los.	*There was not much going on in the discotheque.*
Werner ging mit Tina aus.	*Werner went out with Tina.*
Die Touristen fuhren zum Museum.	*The tourists drove to the museum.*

Oral Practice 13-1

Listen to your CD to hear the following questions. Press "pause" to repeat each one. Then, using the word in parentheses as your cue, respond with **nein,** using the cue word in your response. Cover the correct answers shown on the right. Use them to compare with your own answers. For example:

Kaufte er ein Hemd? (ein Buch)
You say: Nein, er kaufte ein Buch. *No, he bought a book.*

GRAMMAR DEMYSTIFIED

Contractions

German contractions tend to be formed by combining prepositions and articles. Unlike English, German does not require an apostrophe in a contraction. Some examples are:

Preposition and Article	Contraction
an das	ans
an dem	am
bei dem	beim
in das	ins
in dem	im
von dem	vom
zu dem	zum
zu der	zur

Verkaufte er seinen Wagen? (sein Fahrrad)	Nein, er verkaufte sein Fahrrad.
Spielten sie Fußball? (Tennis)	Nein, sie spielten Tennis.
Hatte sie Rockmusik gern? (klassische Musik)	Nein, sie hatte klassische Musik gern.
Kamen sie aus der Schweiz? (Österreich)	Nein, sie kamen aus Österreich.
Lernte er Herrn Keller kennen? (Frau Benz)	Nein, er lernte Frau Benz kennen.
Warst du in der Kunstgallerie? (das Museum)	Nein, ich war im Museum.
Lief ein spanischer Film im Kino? (amerikanisch)	Nein, ein amerikanischer Film lief im Kino.
Brachten Sie ihr ein Geschenk? (er)	Nein, ich brachte ihm ein Geschenk.
Machte sie die Tür zu? (das Fenster)	Nein, sie machte das Fenster zu.
Tanzte Dirk mit seiner Schwester? (seine Tante)	Nein, Dirk tanzte mit seiner Tante.
Bekam Franziska die Einladung? (die Eintrittskarten)	Nein, Franziska bekam die Eintrittskarten.

Gingen die Kinder in die Schule? (die Oper)	Nein, die Kinder gingen in die Oper.
Interessierte sie sich für Sport? (Kunst)	Nein, sie interessierte sich für Kunst.
Fuhren deine Eltern mit dem Bus? (der Zug)	Nein, meine Eltern fuhren mit dem Zug.
Sprachen Sie mit dem Chef? (der Schauspieler)	Nein, ich sprach mit dem Schauspieler.

Oral Practice 13-2

TRACK 24

Listen to your CD to hear sentences in the present tense. Press "pause" and repeat each one. Then restate the sentence in the past tense. Listen to the correct answer on your CD, making sure to repeat what you hear. For example:

Ist diese Einladung für den Lehrer?
You say: War diese Einladung für den Lehrer? *Was this invitation for the teacher?*

Wir spielen gern Fußball.

Ich höre jeden Abend Radio.

Niemand macht das Fenster auf.

Die Jungen gehen in die Kunstgallerie.

Der Tanzklub ist neben dem Museum.

Sie fragt die junge Schauspielerin.

Franziska tanzt gern mit Horst.

Ich habe keine Lust mitzugehen.

Bekommst du die Eintrittskarten?

Wohin fahren deine Gäste?

Lernen die Kinder Deutsch?

Ich bringe ihr fünf gelbe Rosen.

Im Kino läuft ein neuer Film.

Jemand wartet auf uns.

Niemand redet über das Stück.

GRAMMAR DEMYSTIFIED

Prefixes

It's very common to add a prefix to a German verb to change its meaning. Some prefixes are called *inseparable prefixes*, because they remain attached to the verb. Others are called *separable prefixes*, because they are detached from the verb when the verb is conjugated. Some examples are:

Base Verb	**Inseparable Prefix**	**Separable Prefix**
kommen *to come*	bekommen *to receive*	mitkommen *to come along*
stehen *to stand*	verstehen *to understand*	beistehen *to assist, stand by*
schreiben *to write*	beschreiben *to describe*	zuschreiben *to attribute to*
fahren *to drive*	erfahren *to experience*	vorbeifahren *to drive past*

With separable prefixes, notice how the prefix separates from the verb during conjugation, while the inseparable prefixes remain attached:

Inseparable Prefix	**Separable Prefix**
ich bekomme, du bekommst	ich komme mit, du kommst mit
er erfährt, wir erfahren	er fährt vorbei, wir fahren vorbei

The inseparable prefixes are: **be-**, **emp-**, **ent-**, **er-**, **ge-**, **ver-**, and **zer-**. Of the numerous separable prefixes, many are formed from prepositions and adverbs. Some of the most common are: **an-**, **auf-**, **aus-**, **bei-**, **mit-**, **vor-**, **weg-**, **zu-**, and **zurück**.

> **NOTE:** *Separable prefixes are the last element in a sentence:* **Er machte die Tür und die Fenster auf.**

Asking Specific Questions with Interrogatives

You've already encountered a variety of interrogatives that help to introduce questions. They are:

wer, wen, wem, wessen	*who, whom, whose* (inquiring about a person)
was	*what* (inquiring about an object)
wo	*where* (inquiring about location)

wohin	*where (to)* (inquiring about motion or direction)
wie	*how* (inquiring about means or method)
wann	*when* (inquiring about time)
warum	*why* (inquiring about a reason)

If a question is asking about something *in general* and can be responded to by using a yes or no answer, it is a **ja-nein** question. But if a question asks about a specific element in a statement, one of the interrogative words must be used in the question. For example:

Questions in General

Hören Sie Radio? *Are you listening to the radio?*	Ja, ich höre Radio.
Sprechen Sie Deutsch? *Do you speak German?*	Nein, ich spreche Englisch.

Questions About a Specific Element

Was schreiben Sie? *What are you writing?*	Ich schreibe einen Brief.
Wo tanztet ihr? *Where did you dance?*	Wir tanzten im Tanzklub.
Wann war das Fest? *When was the party?*	Das Fest war am Freitag.
Wie läuft Erik? *How does Erik run?*	Erik läuft schnell.

Oral Practice 13-3

 TRACK 25

Listen to your CD to hear a variety of responses to questions. Press "pause" to repeat each one. Then ask the appropriate question based upon the element that is underlined. Listen to the correct answer on your CD, making sure to repeat what you hear. For example:

Ich bekam eine Einladung.
You say: Was bekamst du? *What did you receive?*

Wir spielen gern Fußball.

Niemand wartet auf uns.

Frau Mann fuhr nach Österreich.

Ihr Geburtstag war im Juni.

Meine Gäste kommen aus der Schweiz.

Franziska singt am besten.

Er kommt nicht mit, weil er krank ist.

Tina machte die Tür zu.

Ich lernte Herrn Keller kennen.

Jemand redete über den Künstler.

Karl sprach mit dem Schauspieler.

Der Zug kam um vierzehn Uhr.

Frau Mann muss in der Stadt bleiben.

Die Schauspielerin war sehr jung.

Er verkaufte ihr Haus.

VOCABULARY DEMYSTIFIED

Buildings in Germany

In Germany, the numbering of floors in a building is done a bit differently from how it's done in the United States. The first floor is always called the *ground floor*. Then the numbering starts from there.

In Germany	In the United States
das Erdgeschoss	*ground floor, first floor*
das erste Stock	*second floor*
das zweite Stock	*third floor*
das dritte Stock	*fourth floor*

And so on.

Written Practice 13-1

Fill in each blank with the simple past tense of the verb in parentheses.

1. Er _____________ für einen neuen Chef. (arbeiten)
2. Wo _____________ du? (sein)
3. Niemand _____________ Lust ins Kino zu gehen. (haben)
4. Ich _____________ alle Fenster auf. (machen)
5. Warum _____________ deine Gäste nach Hause? (gehen)

Written Practice 13-2

The following lines of dialogue are out of sequence. Place a number, from 1 to 8, in each blank to show the appropriate order for the lines.

_____ Selbstverständlich. Gibt es eine neue Ausstellung?

_____ Ja, aber die Eintrittskarten sind sehr teuer.

_____ Ich gehe lieber ins Konzert. Es gibt eine Sinfonie von Beethoven.

_____ Schön. Ich gehe immer gern tanzen.

_____ Ja, Werke von einer neuen Künstlerin aus Amerika.

_____ Du hast recht. Interessierst du dich für die Kunst?

_____ Das geht. Aber gehen wir lieber in die Diskothek.

_____ Hast du Lust, heute abend in die Diskothek zu gehen?

PHRASES FOR SURVIVAL

Recreation

Add these useful words and phrases to your language arsenal to help you get by in the German-speaking world:

Um wie viel Uhr wird der Konzertsaal geöffnet?	*What time does the concert hall open?*
Das Schwimmbad schließt um neunzehn Uhr.	*The pool closes at seven* P.M.
der Zirkus	*circus*
das Rennen	*race*
der Zoo	*zoo*
das Konzert	*concert*
Wo ist die Garderobe?	*Where is the cloakroom?*
Gibt es eine Studentenermäßigung?	*Is there a student discount?*

QUIZ

TRACK 26

Responding to questions. Listen to your CD to hear each question. Press "pause" to repeat the question out loud and select your answer—a, b, or c. Then listen to the correct answer on the CD, making sure to repeat what you hear.

1. (a) Morgen früh.
   (b) Heute nachmittag.
   (c) Nächsten Montag.

2. (a) Einen neuen Spielfilm.
   (b) Vier Werke von Picasso.
   (c) Eine Sinfonie von Mozart.

3. (a) Auf dem Fest.
   (b) Sehr gut.
   (c) In der Kunstgallerie.

4. (a) Ja, ich tanzte stundenlang.
   (b) Nein, ich ging nicht zum Tanzklub.
   (c) Ja, ich tanze gern aber nicht gut.

5. (a) Nein, ich interessiere mich für Rockmusik.
   (b) Ja, sie interessiert sich für „Faust".
   (c) Nein, sie hört lieber Jazzmusik.

Using each of the phrases provided, say that *the judge* carried out that action *in the past tense*. Listen to the correct answers on your CD, making sure to repeat what you hear. For example:

einen Anzug kaufen
You say: Der Richter kaufte einen Anzug. *The judge bought a suit.*

6. in der Kunstgallerie sein
7. die Künsterlin gern haben
8. in der Stadt wohnen
9. mit den Kindern spielen
10. das Fenster aufmachen

CHAPTER 14

Home Life

In this chapter you will learn:

Umzugsvorbereitungen *Getting Ready to Move*

Rooms and Furniture

Indicating Location or Movement with Three Verb Pairs

Umzugsvorbereitungen Getting Ready to Move

Listen to the following dialogue on your CD. After you hear a phrase or sentence on a track, always press "pause" and repeat what you hear.

KLAUS: Zwanzig Jahre haben wir in dieser Wohnung gewohnt.	*We have lived in this apartment for twenty years.*
INGE: Zu lange! Wir haben schon seit fünf Jahren ein größeres Haus gebraucht.	*Too long! We have needed a bigger house for five years.*

KLAUS: Das stimmt. Aber hier sind unsere Kinder geboren und Großvater gestorben.	*That is true. But our children were born here and Grandfather died here.*
INGE: Hab keine Angst! Diese Erinnerungen werden mit uns ins neue Haus ziehen.	*Do not worry! These memories will move into the new house along with us.*
KLAUS: Endlich werden wir eine Garage haben. Und einen Blumengarten neben der Terasse.	*We will finally have a garage. And a flower garden next to the terrace.*
INGE: Ich freue mich auf die Geschirrspülmaschine in der neuen Küche.	*I am looking forward to the dishwasher in the new kitchen.*
KLAUS: Wo sind mein Laptop und Handy? Hast du sie schon eingepackt?	*Where are my laptop and cell phone? Did you already pack them?*
INGE: Nein, der Laptop ist noch im Schlafzimmer, und dein Handy liegt auf dem Schreibtisch.	*No, the laptop is still in the bedroom, and your cell phone is on the desk.*
KLAUS: Es klingelt. Die Möbelpacker sind da.	*There is the bell. The movers are here.*

Dialogue Review

Answer the following questions about the dialogue **Umzugsvorbereitungen**. Cover the correct answers shown on the right. Use them to compare with your own answers.

1. Wie lange haben Klaus und Inge in ihrer Wohnung gewohnt? *How long have Klaus and Inge lived in their apartment?*	Sie haben zwanzig Jahre in ihrer Wohnung gewohnt.
2. Woran erinnert sich Klaus? *What does Klaus remember?*	Er erinnert sich an die Geburt seiner Kinder und den Tod seines Großvaters.

3. Was werden sie im neuen Haus haben? *What will they have in the new house?* — Sie werden eine Garage und einen Blumengarten haben.

4. Worauf freut sich Inge? *What is Inge looking forward to?* — Inge freut sich auf die Geschirrspülmaschine in der neuen Küche.

5. Hat Inge das Handy schon eingepackt? *Did Inge already pack the cell phone?* — Nein, das Handy liegt noch auf dem Schreibtisch.

ROOMS AND FURNITURE

When moving in or out of a house or apartment, there are many important words and phrases that help get the job done. It is important to know the words for packing, for the rooms where the furniture is to be located, and for the furniture itself. Let's get acquainted with some of this vocabulary.

TRACK 28

Listen to your CD to hear the following sentences. Press "pause" after each sentence and repeat what you hear.

Wir kaufen neue Möbel.	*We are buying new furniture.*
Wir sind gerade dabei, unsere Wohnung zu renovieren.	*We are redecorating our apartment.*
Wir sind noch nicht verkabelt.	*We still do not have cable.*
Im Wohnzimmer haben sie ein Sofa.	*They have a sofa in the living room.*
Im Wohnzimmer haben sie zwei Sessel.	*They have two armchairs in the living room.*
Im Wohnzimmer haben sie einen Fernsehapparat.	*They have a TV in the living room.*
Das Haus ist schon frisch gestrichen.	*The house is already freshly painted.*

Ich suche neue Tapeten für den Flur aus.	*I am looking for new wallpaper for the hallway.*
Unser Haus war zu klein und wir mussten anbauen.	*Our house was too little, and we had to put on an addition.*
Im Esszimmer steht ein runder Esstisch.	*There is a round dining table in the dining room.*
Im Esszimmer stehen vier Stühle.	*There are four chairs in the dining room.*
Herr Keller will ein Grundstück in ruhiger Lage.	*Mr. Keller wants a lot in a quiet neighborhood.*
Wir haben den Teppichboden selbst verlegt.	*We laid the carpet ourselves.*
In unserem Schlafzimmer gibt es zwei Betten.	*There are two beds in our bedroom.*
Im Schlafzimmer gibt es einen Kleiderschrank.	*There is a wardrobe in the bedroom.*
Ihre Wohnung befindet sich in einem Hochhaus.	*Their apartment is in a high-rise.*
In der Küche haben wir einen Kühlschrank.	*We have a refrigerator in the kitchen.*
In der Küche haben wir noch keinen Herd.	*We still do not have a range in the kitchen.*
Das Badezimmer ist neben dem Flur.	*The bathroom is next to the hallway.*
Sein Haus hat einen Keller und einen Dachboden.	*His house has a basement and an attic.*

Notice that German has a variety of ways to say which pieces of furniture are in a room: **wir haben** (*we have*), **es gibt** (*there is/are*), and **etwas steht** (*something is standing*). When you use **es gibt**, don't forget that the *accusative case* is required.

In der Küche gibt es <u>einen</u> Tisch.	*There is a table in the kitchen.*
Im Flur gibt es <u>einen</u> Kleiderschrank.	*There is a wardrobe in the hallway.*

Notice, too, how the base word **der Schrank** (*cabinet*) is used to form the new words **der Kleiderschrank** (*wardrobe*) and **der Kühlschrank** (*refrigerator*).

GRAMMAR DEMYSTIFIED

Reflexive Pronouns

German often adds a reflexive pronoun to a sentence in order to complete the meaning of a verb. English does the same thing, but not with the same frequency as German. The German reflexive pronouns are **mich**, **dich**, **sich**, **uns**, and **euch**. Let's look at how they function in some sample sentences:

sich freuen

Ich freue mich darauf.	*I am looking forward to it.*
Du freust dich darauf.	*You are looking forward to it.*
Er/Sie/Es freut sich darauf.	*He/She/It is looking forward to it.*
Wir freuen uns darauf.	*We are looking forward to it.*
Ihr freut euch darauf.	*You are looking forward to it.*
Sie freuen sich darauf.	*You are looking forward to it.*
Sie freuen sich darauf.	*They are looking forward to it.*

sich setzen

Ich setze mich neben Karl.	*I seat myself next to Karl.*
Du setzt dich neben Karl.	*You seat yourself next to Karl.*
Er/Sie/Es setzt sich neben Karl.	*He/She/It seats himself/herself/itself next to Karl.*
Wir setzen uns neben Karl.	*We seat ourselves next to Karl.*
Ihr setzt euch neben Karl.	*You seat yourselves next to Karl.*
Sie setzen sich neben Karl.	*You seat yourself next to Karl.*
Sie setzen sich neben Karl.	*They seat themselves next to Karl.*

Oral Practice 14-1

TRACK 29

Listen to the questions on your CD. Press "pause" to repeat each one. Then, using the cue provided in parentheses, tell where the object specified in the question is located. Listen to the correct answer on your CD, making sure to repeat what you hear. For example:

> Wo gibt es einen Tisch? (*kitchen*)
> *You say*: In der Küche gibt es einen Tisch. *There is a table in the kitchen.*

Wo habt ihr ein Radio? (*bedroom*)

Wo steht dein Wagen? (*garage*)

Wo gibt es einen Sessel? (*living room*)

Wo hast du einen Kleiderschrank? (*bedroom*)

Wo gibt es einen Schreibtisch? (*living room*)

Wo steht der Kühlschrank? (*kitchen*)

Wo habt ihr vier Stühle? (*dining room*)

Wo gibt es eine Geschirrspülmaschine? (*kitchen*)

Wo steht das Bett? (*bedroom*)

Wo habt ihr einen alten Esstisch? (*basement*)

Wo gibt es neue Tapeten? (*hallway*)

Wo steht das Sofa? (*living room*)

Indicating Location or Movement with Three Verb Pairs

There are three pairs of verbs that require a little explanation. One of the verbs in each pair is followed by the accusative case with certain prepositions, and the other verb is followed by the dative case with the same prepositions. These prepositions are **an** (*at*), **auf** (*on*), **hinter** (*behind*), **in** (*in*), **neben** (*next to*), **über** (*over*), **unter** (*under*), **vor** (*before*), and **zwischen** (*between*).

The verb pairs are **legen/liegen** (*lay, lie*), **stellen/stehen** (*place, stand*), and **setzen/sitzen** (*set, sit*). Notice that each of the pairs describes a position: lying flat,

standing upright, and being in a sitting position. The first verb in each pair describes a *movement* to a place. The second verb shows a *location*. If there is movement (**legen**, **stellen**, **setzen**), use the accusative case with the prepositions described previously. If there is location (**liegen**, **stehen**, **sitzen**), use the dative case. For example:

Ich lege das Buch auf den Tisch.	*I lay the book on the table.*
Das Buch liegt auf dem Tisch.	*The book lies on the table.*
Er stellt den Regenschirm in den Schrank.	*He places the umbrella in the cabinet.*
Der Regenschirm steht im Schrank.	*The umbrella is (standing) in the cabinet.*
Ich setze mich neben meinen Freund.	*I seat myself next to my friend.*
Ich sitze neben meinem Freund.	*I sit next to my friend.*

Oral Practice 14-2

TRACK 30

Read each question out loud. Then, using the word in parentheses as your cue, respond with **nein** putting the cue word in your response. Cover the correct answers shown on the right, listen to them on the CD, and repeat what you hear. For example:

Hast du das Buch auf den Tisch gelegt? (Stuhl)	*Did you lay the book on the table?*
You say: Nein, das Buch liegt schon auf dem Stuhl.	*No, the book is already (lying) on the chair.*

Hast du die Vase auf den Stuhl gestellt? (Tisch)	Nein, die Vase steht schon auf dem Tisch.
Hast du die Zeitung auf den Stuhl gelegt? (Sofa)	Nein, die Zeitung liegt schon auf dem Sofa.
Hat er sich neben Klaus gesetzt? (Tina)	Nein, er sitzt schon neben Tina.
Hat er sich zwischen die Jungen gesetzt? (seine Eltern)	Nein, er sitzt schon zwischen seinen Eltern.

Hat sie das Baby auf den Sessel gelegt? (Bett)	Nein, das Baby liegt schon auf dem Bett.
Haben Sie die Lampe neben den Herd gestellt? (Esstisch)	Nein, die Lampe steht schon neben dem Esstisch.
Hat er sich an das Fenster gestellt? (Tür)	Nein, er steht schon an der Tür.
Hat sie die Handschuhe unter den Tisch gelegt? (Bett)	Nein, die Handschuhe liegen schon unter dem Bett.
Haben Sie sich vor Ihren Bruder gesetzt? (Onkel)	Nein, ich sitze schon vor meinem Onkel.
Hast du den Kuchen in den Schrank gestellt? (Kühlschrank)	Nein, der Kuchen steht schon im Kühlschrank.

GRAMMAR DEMYSTIFIED

Asking a Question with a Preposition

When asking a question with a preposition, the preposition precedes **wen** (accusative case) or **wem** (dative case) when the object of the preposition is a person. For example:

Auf wen wartest du?	*For whom are you waiting?/Who are you waiting for?*
Mit wem tanzt er?	*With whom does he dance?/Who does he dance with?*

If the object of the preposition is an inanimate object, the prefix **wo-** is added to the preposition. If the preposition begins with a vowel, the prefix is **wor-**. For example:

Worauf freust du dich?	*What are you looking forward to?*
Wovon sprecht ihr?	*What are you talking about?*

If the inanimate object is a *location* or a *time*, **wo** and **wann** tend to replace the **wo-** + preposition construction.

Statement	Question	
Sie ist in der Garage.	Wo ist sie?	*She is in the garage. Where is she?*
Karl kommt am Freitag.	Wann kommt Karl?	*Karl is coming Friday. When is Karl coming?*

Oral Practice 14-3

TRACK 31

Read each sentence out loud. Then, using the underlined word or phrase as your cue, ask the appropriate question. Cover the correct answers shown on the right, listen to them on the CD, and repeat what you hear. For example:

Ich warte auf den Zug.
You say: Worauf wartest du? *What are you waiting for?*

Er interessiert sich für Deutsch.	Wofür interessiert er sich?
Er redet über das Buch.	Worüber redet er?
Inge schreibt mit einem Bleistift.	Womit schreibt Inge?
Klaus denkt oft an seine Probleme.	Woran denkt Klaus oft?
Ich sitze neben dem Fernsehapparat.	Woneben sitzt du?
Seine Freundin steht vor der Tür.	Wovor steht seine Freundin?
Der Hund schläft unter dem Tisch.	Worunter schläft der Hund?
Der Zug fährt durch den Tunnel.	Wodurch fährt der Zug?
Der Chef fragte nach dem Konzert.	Wonach fragte der Chef?
Sie freuen sich auf das Geschirrspülmaschine.	Worauf freuen sie sich?

Written Practice 14-1

Fill in each blank with the appropriate reflexive pronoun.

1. Er freut _______________ auf das neue Haus.
2. Du kannst _______________ neben Frau Keller setzen.
3. Ich stellte _______________ ans Fenster.
4. Wir haben _______________ sehr darauf gefreut.
5. Freuen Sie _______________ nicht darauf?

VOCABULARY DEMYSTIFIED

The Metric System

Since Europe uses the metric system, it's important to have an idea of the differences between that system and the English/American system of measurement. Some examples are:

Dieser Krug enthält einen Liter.	*This mug contains one liter.*	*2.11 pints*
Die Flasche enthält fünf Liter Milch.	*The bottle contains five liters of milk.*	*5.28 gallons*
Es wiegt zehn Gramm.	*It weighs ten grams.*	*.4 ounces*
Das Paket wiegt ein Kilogramm.	*The package weighs one kilogram.*	*2.2 pounds*
Es hat eine Länge von zehn Zentimetern.	*Its length is ten centimeters.*	*3.9 inches*
Die Höhe ist ein Meter.	*The height is one meter.*	*1.09 yards*
Das Dorf ist ein Kilometer von hier entfernt.	*The village is one kilometer from here*	*.62 miles*

When a German says **Pfund** (*pound*), the quantity is 500 grams or half a kilogram and not the same pound measurement as in the United States: **drei Pfund Butter** (*three pounds of butter*) = *1.5 kilograms.*

To convert kilometers to miles, divide by 8 and multiply by 5. To convert miles to kilometers, divide by 5 and multiply by 8.

Speed limits are usually shown in their abbreviated form: **80 km/h** = **achtzig Kilometer pro Stunde** (*eighty kilometers per hour*).

Germans use the **Celsius** (*centigrade*) thermometer. Take a look at some Celsius temperature readings compared to the Fahrenheit thermometer:

Celsius	**Fahrenheit**
100 (boiling temperature)	212
36.9 (body temperature)	98.4
0 (freezing temperature)	32
–20	–4

To convert Celsius to Fahrenheit, divide by 5, multiply by 9, then add 32. To convert Fahrenheit to Celsius, subtract 32, divide by 9, and multiply by 5.

CULTURE DEMYSTIFIED

German Homes

Homes and apartments in Germany are generally described by the number of rooms they have or in their number of square meters.

Das ist eine Fünf-Zimmer-Wohnung. *This is a five-room apartment.*

This kind of statement is often abbreviated:

Das ist eine 5-Zi.-Whg.

Or one might say:

Es hat ungefähr hundertzehn Quadratmeter. *It has about 110 square meters.*

This statement can also be abbreviated:

Es hat ca. 110 m^2. (ca. = circa, m^2 = Quadratmeter)

Written Practice 14-2

The following lines of dialogue are out of sequence. Place a number, from 1 to 8, in each blank to show the appropriate order for the lines.

_____ Ich freue mich auf den neuen Herd und den Kühlschrank.

_____ Achtzehn Jahre. Aber wir hätten schon vor fünf Jahren ein größeres Haus kaufen sollen.

_____ Diese Erinnerungen werden mit uns ins neue Haus ziehen.

_____ Nein, es liegt auf dem Bett im Schlafzimmer.

_____ Aber vergiss nicht, dass Werner und Tina hier geboren sind.

_____ Das neue Haus hat keine Garage aber einen schönen Blumengarten.

_____ Hast du mein Handy schon eingepackt?

_____ Wie viele Jahre haben wir in dieser Wohnung gewohnt?

PHRASES FOR SURVIVAL

Having Fun

Add these useful phrases to your language arsenal to help you get by in the German-speaking world:

Es macht Spaß.	*It is fun.*
Das ist kein Spaß.	*That is no fun.*
Viel Spaß!	*Have fun!*
Die Schule macht mir Spaß.	*I enjoy school./School is fun for me.*
Umzüge machen uns keinen Spaß.	*Moving is no fun for us.*
Verdirb ihm doch nicht seinen Spaß!	*Do not spoil his fun!*

The preposition **vor** can be used to mean *ago.* For example:

Sie ist vor zehn Jahren geboren.	*She was born ten years ago.*
Vor zwei Monaten wohnte ich in dieser Wohnung.	*Two months ago I lived in this apartment.*

QUIZ

 TRACK 32

Responding to questions. Listen to Track 38 to hear each question. Press "pause" to repeat the question out loud and select your answer—a, b, or c. Then listen to the correct answer on your CD, making sure to repeat what you hear.

1. (a) Ja, das Handy ist auf dem Tisch.
   (b) Nein, er ist im Wohnzimmer.
   (c) Die Möbelpacker sind schon da.

2. (a) Das Krankenhaus ist sehr weit von hier.
   (b) Er ist im Juni gestorben.
   (c) Er freut sich auf die neue Garage.

3. (a) Nein, ans Fenster.
   (b) Ja, neben der Terasse.
   (c) Nein, aufs Bett.

4. (a) Zwischen dem Sessel und dem Schrank.
   (b) Unter dem Esstisch.
   (c) Er steht zwischen seinen Eltern.

5. (a) Nein, der Kühlschrank ist in der Küche.
   (b) Im Esszimmer haben wir sechs Stühle.
   (c) Im Schlafzimmer haben wir einen Schreibtisch und ein Bett.

Using the words provided as your cues, say that in the location given there is that piece of furniture. Listen to the correct answers on your CD, making sure to repeat what you hear. For example:

> Wohnzimmer, Sofa
> *You say*: Im Wohnzimmer gibt es ein Sofa. *There is a sofa in the living room.*

6. Küche, Herd
7. Schlafzimmer, Schreibtisch
8. Esszimmer, vier Stühle
9. Flur, Kleiderschrank
10. Keller, Kühlschrank

CHAPTER 15

Staying Informed

In this chapter you will learn:

Reading Zeitungen und Zeitschriften *(Newspapers and Magazines)*

Television and Print Media

Reading *Zeitungen und Zeitschriften* (Newspapers and Magazines)

 TRACK 33

Listen to the following dialogue on your CD. After you hear a phrase or sentence on a track, always press "pause" and repeat what you hear.

SIGRID: Du liest jeden Morgen Zeitung. Kannst du nicht ein paar Worte mit mir reden?	*You read the newspaper every morning. Can't you say a few words to me?*
HANS: Man muss die Zeitung lesen um informiert zu sein.	*You have to read the newspaper to be informed.*

SIGRID: Ich finde Zeitschriften viel interessanter. Und ich lerne sehr viel dabei.	*I think magazines are a lot more interesting. And I learn a lot at the same time.*
HANS: Die Zeitung ist ausführlicher als eine Zeitschrift und sogar als die Nachrichten im Fernsehen oder im Internet.	*The newspaper is more detailed than a magazine and even the news on TV or on the Internet.*
SIGRID: Gar nicht der Fall! Und im Fernsehen kann man ausgezeichnete Dokumentarfilme sehen.	*That is not the case at all! And you can watch excellent documentaries on TV.*
HANS: Lieber eine Meldung vom Sport. Oder die Übertragung der Fußballmeisterschaft.	*Preferably a sports report. Or the broadcast of the soccer championship.*
SIGRID: Zum Informieren sind all die Medien. wichtig.	*All the media are important for keeping people informed.*
HANS: Ich habe beinahe vergessen. Heute spielen Hamburg und Düsseldorf. Wo ist die Fernbedienung?	*I almost forgot. Hamburg and Düsseldorf play today. Where is the remote?*

Dialogue Review

Answer the following questions about the dialogue Reading **Zeitungen und Zeitschriften**. Cover the correct answers shown on the right. Use them to compare with your own answers.

1. Warum reden sie nicht miteinander? *Why aren't they talking to each other?*	Hans liest jeden Morgen Zeitung.
2. Was findet Sigrid interessanter? *What does Sigrid find more interesting?*	Sie findet Zeitschriften interessanter.
3. Als was ist die Zeitung ausführlicher? *What is the newspaper more detailed than?*	Sie ist ausführlicher als eine Zeitschrift oder als die Nachrichten im Fernsehen und im Internet.

4. Was kann man im Fernsehen sehen? — Im Fernsehen kann man ausgezeichnete Dokumentarfilme sehen.
   What can you watch on television?

5. Warum sucht Hans die Fernbedienung? — Heute spielen Hamburg und Düsseldorf.
   Why is Hans looking for the remote control?

Note that the German pronoun **man** (*one*) is used where the tendency in the English translation is to use the less formal *you*.

Man muss informiert sein.	*You have to be informed.*
Man kann Dokumentarfilme sehen.	*You can see documentaries.*

GRAMMAR DEMYSTIFIED

-ieren Verbs

There are some verbs in German that end in **-ieren**. Many of these verbs come from a foreign source and are often similar to verbs in English of the same meaning. They are conjugated like regular verbs in German except that in the perfect tenses they require no **ge-** prefix. Here are a few important **-ieren** verbs to know:

studieren *to study*	fotografieren *to photograph*
interessieren *to interest*	diskutieren *to discuss*
protestieren *to protest*	explodieren *to explode*
schockieren *to shock*	reparieren *to repair*

The conjugation of **-ieren** verbs in the various tenses looks like this:

	arrangieren	**marschieren**	
Present	ich arrangiere	er marschiert	*I arrange, he marches*
Past	ich arrangierte	er marschierte	*I arranged, he marched*
Present perfect	ich habe arrangiert	er ist marschiert	*I have arranged, he has marched*
Future	ich werde arrangieren	er wird marschieren	*I will arrange, he will march*

Television and Print Media

TRACK 34

Listen to your CD to hear the following sentences that discuss different forms of media. Press "pause" after each sentence and repeat what you hear.

Ich habe eine Zeitung abonniert.	*I subscribed to a newspaper.*
Der Journalist hat eine Zeitschrift abonniert.	*The journalist subscribed to a magazine.*
Wir haben ein Abonnement fürs Theater.	*We have season tickets to the theater.*
Habt ihr ein Abonnement für die Oper?	*Do you have season tickets for the opera?*
Der Bericht wurde gestern veröffentlicht.	*The report was published yesterday.*
Ihr neuer Roman wird morgen veröffentlicht.	*Her new novel will be published tomorrow.*
Viel Reklame wird dafür gemacht.	*A lot of advertising is being done for it.*
Mein Enkel darf sich nur Kindersendungen ansehen.	*My grandson is allowed to watch only children's shows.*
In welchem Programm kommt die Kindersendung?	*What channel is the children's show on?*
Der Spielfilm kommt in einem anderen Programm.	*The feature film is on another channel.*
Schalte ins zweite Programm um!	*Switch to channel two.*
Ich werde den Krimi im dritten Programm aufnehmen.	*I will record the detective story on channel three.*
Sigrid arbeitete in einem Aufnahmestudio.	*Sigrid worked in a recording studio.*

Was steht für heute abend im Fernsehprogramm? — *What is in the TV guide this evening?*

Steht das Wort nicht in deinem Wörterbuch? — *Isn't that word in your dictionary?*

Note that the verb **kommen** (*to come*) is used with TV channels to mean *on* a particular channel: **Der Film kommt im ersten Programm**. *The film is on channel one*. And the verb **stehen** (*to stand*) is used with written material to say that something is *in* a particular publication: **Das Fernsehprogramm steht jeden Tag in der Zeitung**. *The TV guide is in the newspaper every day.*

Oral Practice 15-1

TRACK 35

Listen to the sentences on your CD. Press "pause" to repeat each one. Then, using the cue provided in parentheses, restate the sentence appropriately. Listen to the correct answer, making sure to repeat what you hear. For example:

Die Kindersendung kommt im zweiten Programm. — *(feature film)*

You say: Der Spielfilm kommt im zweiten Programm. — *The feature film is on channel two.*

Wir haben eine Zeitung abonniert. (*magazine*)

Wir haben ein Abonnement für die Oper. (*theater*)

Ich habe ein Abonnement für die Oper. (*concert*)

Der Bericht wurde gestern veröffentlicht. (*novel*)

Die Reklame wurde gestern veröffentlicht. (*detective story*)

Sie sieht sich die Kindersendung an. (*documentaries*)

Ich sehe mir den Spielfilm an. (*news*)

Der Wetterbericht steht in der Zeitung. (*TV guide*)

Das Kinoprogramm steht in der Zeitung. (*news*)

Der Film kommt im zweiten Programm. (*channel one*)

GRAMMAR DEMYSTIFIED

Pronoun Replacement

When an animate noun is the object of a preposition and is changed to a pronoun, the pronoun must be in the same case as designated by the preposition. For example:

Noun	**Pronoun Replacement**
Sie spricht von ihrem Vater.	Sie spricht von ihm.
Alle reden über die Frau.	Alle reden über sie.

But when the object of a preposition is an inanimate noun, a pronoun cannot replace the noun. Instead, a new structure is formed: the prefix **da-** is added to the preposition and this new word serves as the prepositional phrase with a pronoun. If the preposition begins with a vowel, the prefix used is **dar-**. For example:

Sie spricht von dem Problem.	*Sie spricht davon.*
Alle reden über den Spielfilm.	*Alle reden darüber.*

Oral Practice 15-2

TRACK 36

Read each sentence out loud. Then, restate the sentence, changing the noun in the underlined prepositional phrase appropriately. Cover the correct answers shown on the right, listen to them on the CD, and repeat what you hear. For example:

Das Buch liegt auf dem Bett. *You say*: Das Buch liegt darauf.	*The book is lying on the bed.* *The book is lying on it.*
Steht der Artikel in der Zeitung?	Steht der Artikel darin?
Wir haben auf Herrn Keller gewartet.	Wir haben auf ihn gewartet.
Niemand redet über die Kindersendung.	Niemand redet darüber.
Wir haben ein Abonnement für die Oper.	Wir haben ein Abonnement dafür.
Das ist ein Bericht über meine Freundin.	Das ist ein Bericht über sie.

Diese Zeitschrift ist für meinen Enkel.	Diese Zeitschrift ist für ihn.
Er redete ein paar Worte mit seiner Frau.	Er redete ein paar Worte mit ihr.
Viel Reklame wird für diesen Roman gemacht.	Viel Reklame wird dafür gemacht.
Er repariert die Uhr für Frau Mann.	Er repariert die Uhr für sie.
Ich denke an meinen kranken Onkel.	Ich denke an ihn.
Der Chef fragte nach meinen Kindern.	Der Chef fragte nach ihnen.
Diskutiert ihr über die Sendung?	Diskutiert ihr darüber?
Und hier eine Meldung vom Sport.	Und hier eine Meldung davon.
Kommst du auch mit dem Bus?	Kommst du auch damit?
Er informiert sich über den neuen Richter.	Er informiert sich über ihn.

GRAMMAR DEMYSTIFIED

Using the Phrase *um ... zu*

When using the phrase **um ... zu** (*in order to . . .*), **um** is not being used as a preposition but rather as a conjunction. It combines an introductory sentence with the one that follows. For example:

Ich muss die Zeitung lesen um informiert zu sein.	*I have to read the newspaper (in order) to be informed.*

The last elements of an **um ... zu** phrase will be the word **zu** followed by an infinitive.

Er bleibt zu Hause um seiner Mutter zu helfen.	*He stays home in order to help his mother.*
Wir arbeiten um Geld zu verdienen.	*We work in order to earn money.*
Hans ging zur Party um mit Sigrid zu tanzen.	*Hans went to the party in order to dance with Sigrid.*

If the infinitive has an inseparable prefix, **zu** will stand between the prefix and the rest of the verb: **ansehen** → **anzusehen**, **mitkommen** → **mitzukommen**.

Oral Practice 15-3

Listen to the sentences on Track 43. Press "pause" to repeat each one. Then, using the phrase provided in parentheses, restate the sentence using the new phrase in an **um ... zu** clause. Listen to the correct answer on your CD, making sure to repeat what you hear. For example:

Ich komme nach Bremen. (Ich besuche meine Tante.)
You say: Ich komme nach Bremen um meine Tante zu besuchen. — *I am coming to Bremen (in order) to visit my aunt.*

Ich komme nach Bremen. (Ich arbeite im Aufnahmestudio.)

Sie kommt nach Bremen. (Sie studiert hier Deutsch.)

Wir kommen nach Bremen. (Wir sehen uns einen Spielfilm an.)

Er kauft sich ein Programm. (Er weiß die Namen der Sänger.)

Sie kaufen sich ein Programm. (Sie verstehen die Oper.)

Ich ging ins Kaufhaus. (Ich kaufe einen Fernsehapparat.)

Er ging zur Post. (Er schickt Sigrid einen Brief.)

Wir fahren in die Stadt. (Wir gehen in die Oper.)

Sie schaltet ins zweite Programm um. (Sie sieht einen Dokumentarfilm.)

Ich höre die Nachrichten. (Ich bin informiert.)

Written Practice 15-1

Fill in the blanks with the appropriate pronoun replacement of the noun in each prepositional phrase provided in parentheses.

1. Er freut sich _______________ . (auf das neue Haus)
2. Sie kann _______________ sitzen. (neben Herrn Keller)
3. Jemand steht _______________ . (an der Tür)
4. Man soll nicht _______________ sprechen. (über ihre Probleme)
5. Wir müssen _______________ warten. (auf Sigrid und Hans)

VOCABULARY DEMYSTIFIED

Television

The verb used to say that you are watching television in German seems a bit awkward to an English speaker. English uses a verb followed by a noun: to watch television. In German, there is just a single verb to conjugate: **fernsehen** (*to watch television*).

Ich sehe jeden Morgen fern.	*I watch television every morning.*
Wir sahen heute abend fern.	*We watched television this evening.*
Warum hast du so oft ferngesehen?	*Why did you watch television so often?*
Die Kinder werden heute nicht fernsehen.	*The children will not watch television today.*

Written Practice 15-2

The following lines of dialogue are out of sequence. Place a number, from 1 to 8, in each blank to show the appropriate order for the lines.

_____ Um informiert zu sein.

_____ Morgen kannst du darüber in der Zeitung lesen.

_____ Aber es gibt eine Übertragung der Fußballmeisterschaft.

_____ Ich sehe mir das Spiel lieber im Fernsehen an.

_____ Warum siehst du wieder fern? Kannst du nicht ein paar Worte mit mir reden?

_____ Die Sendung beginnt. Wo ist die Fernbedienung?

_____ Immer Sport! Im Fernsehen kannst du auch ausgezeichnete Dokumentarfilme sehen.

_____ Warum soll ich mir Dokumentarfilme ansehen?

PHRASES FOR SURVIVAL

Communications

Add these useful words and phrases to your language arsenal to help you get by in the German-speaking world:

Ich lese gern englische Zeitungen.	*I like reading English newspapers.*
die Illustrierte	*magazine*
das Taschenbuch	*paperback book*
der Kiosk	*newsstand*
Ich habe eine E-Mail von ihr bekommen.	*I got an e-mail from her.*
Sind Sie jetzt verkabelt?	*Do you have cable TV now?*

QUIZ

 **TRACK 38**

Responding to questions. Listen to Track 44 to hear each question. Press "pause" to repeat the question out loud and select your answer—a, b, or c. Then listen to the correct answer on the CD, making sure to repeat what you hear.

1. (a) Ja, die Fernbedienung ist im Wohnzimmer.
   (b) Nein, zwei Zeitschriften.
   (c) Ja, eine Oper von Mozart.

2. (a) Den neuen Fernsehapparat.
   (b) Eine neue Kindersendung.
   (c) Diese neue Fernbedienung.

3. (a) Die Fußballmeisterschaft.
   (b) Ich habe das Fernsehprogramm.
   (c) Im dritten Programm.

4. (a) Im Fernsehen.
   (b) Ich bin darauf abonniert.
   (c) Einen Krimi.

5. (a) Nein, sie fährt nie damit.
   (b) Ja, sie fahren ins Konzert.
   (c) Nein, das Theater ist sehr weit von hier.

Using the word or phrase provided as your cue, say that *there is a broadcast* of that program today. Listen to the correct answers on your CD, making sure to repeat what you hear. For example:

die Fußballmeisterschaft
You say: Heute gibt es eine Übertragung der Fußballmeisterschaft. *There is a broadcast of the soccer championship today.*

6. ein Tennisspiel
7. eine Oper
8. das Fußballspiel
9. das Ballett
10. eine Sinfonie von Brahms

FINAL TEST

TRACK 39

Responding to questions. Listen to your CD to hear each question. Press "pause" to repeat the question out loud and select your answer—a, b, or c. Then listen to the correct answer on the CD, making sure to repeat what you hear.

1. (a) Die Schwester meiner Freundin.
   (b) Die Kinder seines Freundes.
   (c) Sabines Sohn.

2. (a) Der Sohn des Richters schläft noch.
   (b) Sie schenkte ihr einen Pulli.
   (c) Sie war nicht müde und arbeitet noch.

3. (a) Eines Freundes.
   (b) Ein Freund.
   (c) Einem Freund.

4. (a) Sie möchte ein neues Hemd.
   (b) Sein Vater möchte ein weißes Hemd.
   (c) Ich möchte ein rotes Hemd.

5. (a) Ein Bus.
   (b) Das Krankenhaus und der Bahnhof.
   (c) Er kommt aus Frankreich.

6. (a) Ich muss mit euch sprechen.
   (b) Er kann nicht sprechen.
   (c) Wir möchten mit dem Chef sprechen.

7. (a) Gestern abend.
   (b) Vor zwei Tagen.
   (c) Nächsten Montag.

8. (a) Ein neues Kinoprogramm.
   (b) Ein Künstler aus der Schweiz.
   (c) Eine Sinfonie von Beethoven.

9. (a) Auf dem Fest.
   (b) In der Oper.
   (c) Ausgezeichnet.

10. (a) Ja, der Laptop ist auf dem Tisch.
    (b) Nein, es liegt noch auf dem Bett.
    (c) Die Möbelpacker kommen am Freitag.

11. (a) Ja, ich habe oft von euch gesprochen.
    (b) Alle werden mit uns reden.
    (c) Nein, ich habe nicht davon gesprochen.

12. (a) Mit dem Mädchen aus Amerika.
    (b) Eine neue Sportsendung.
    (c) Wo ist die Fernbedienung?

13. (a) Die Fußballmeisterschaft.
    (b) Ich habe die Fernbedienung.
    (c) Im ersten Programm.

14. (a) Morgen früh.
    (b) Gestern nachmittag.
    (c) Nächsten März.

15. (a) Nein, der Kühlschrank ist in der Küche.
    (b) Im Esszimmer haben wir sechs Stühle.
    (c) Da haben wir ein Sofa und einen Sessel.

Using the word or phrase provided as your cue, say that *Tina photographs* that person or object. Listen to the correct answers on your CD, making sure to repeat what you hear. For example:

female teacher
You say: Tina fotografiert die Lehrerin.

16. *museum*
17. *train station*
18. *doctor*
19. *apartment*
20. *actor*

Using the phrase provided as your cue, say that *no one* carried out that action, using *the simple past tense.* Listen to the correct answers on your CD, making sure to repeat what you hear. For example:

einen Anzug kaufen
You say: Niemand kaufte einen Anzug. *No one bought a suit.*

21. in der Kunstgallerie sein
22. seinen Freund gern haben
23. in dieser Wohnung wohnen
24. darauf warten
25. die Tür aufmachen

ENGLISH-GERMAN DICTIONARY

a, an ein, eine

address Adresse (*f.*)

to admire bewundern

to adopt adoptieren

after nach

afterward nachdem

against gegen

against wider

airplane Flugzeug (*n.*)

airport Flughafen (*m.*)

all alle

alone allein

along entlang

Alps Alpen (*pl.*)

already schon

always immer

America Amerika

American Amerikaner (*m.*)

and und

angry, mad böse

to annoy, irritate reizen

to answer antworten

apartment Wohnung (*f.*)

apothecary Apotheke (*f.*)

April April (*m.*)

Arabic arabisch

architect Architekt (*m.*)

arm Arm (*m.*)

around um

to arrange arrangieren

to arrest verhaften

to arrive ankommen

as als

to ask fragen

to astound erstaunen

at an

at home zu Hause

athlete Sportler (*m.*)

attractive attraktiv

August August (*m.*)

aunt Tante (*f.*)

Australia Australien

Austria Österreich
autumn Herbst (*m.*)
bad schlecht
to bake backen
baker Bäcker (*m.*)
ball Ball (*m.*)
ballpoint pen Kuli (*m.*)
bank Bank (*f.*)
baron Freiherr (*m.*)
baroness Freifrau (*f.*)
to be sein
to be acquainted with kennen
to be called, named heißen
to be pleased, glad sich freuen
to be valid, worth gelten
to be wrong sich irren
to bear (a child) gebären
bear Bär (*m.*)
because denn, weil
because of wegen
to become, get; shall/will werden
bed Bett (*n.*)
beef Rindfleisch (*n.*)
beer Bier (*n.*)
before, in front of vor
behind hinter
to believe glauben
to belong to gehören
belt Gürtel (*m.*)
berry Beere (*f.*)
between zwischen
beverage Getränk (*n.*)
bicycle Fahrrad (*n.*)
big groß
billion Milliarde (*f.*)
black schwarz
blind blind
blouse Bluse (*f.*)
book Buch (*n.*)
boss Chef (*m.*)
bottle Flasche (*f.*)
bouquet Blumenstrauß (*m.*)
boy Junge (*m.*)
bread Brot (*n.*)
to break brechen
bricklayer Maurer (*m.*)
bridge Brücke (*f.*)
bright hell
to bring bringen
brother Bruder (*m.*)
brown braun
bus Bus (*m.*)
bush Busch (*m.*)
businessman Geschäftsmann (*m.*)
businesswoman Geschäftsfrau (*f.*)
but aber
butcher Metzger (*m.*)
to buy kaufen
by bei
by heart auswendig

cabbage Kohl (*m.*)
to call up, telephone anrufen
calm, quiet ruhig
Canada Kanada
capital city Hauptstadt (*f.*)
capitalist Kapitalist (*m.*)
car Auto (*n.*)
car Wagen (*m.*)
carnation Nelke (*f.*)
carpet Teppich (*m.*)
castle Burg (*f.*)
cat Katze (*f.*)
cathedral Dom (*m.*)
CD CD (*f.*)
chair Stuhl (*m.*)
chalk Kreide (*f.*)
chancellor Kanzler (*m.*)
to change ändern
cheap billig
cheese Käse (*m.*)
chemist Chemiker (*m.*)
chess Schach (*n.*)
chicken Hühnchen (*n.*)
chicken Huhn (*n.*)
child Kind (*n.*)
church Kirche (*f.*)
circus Zirkus (*m.*)
city center, downtown Stadtzentrum (*n.*)
city excursion Stadtrundfahrt (*f.*)
city hall Rathaus (*n.*)
city Stadt (*f.*)
city wall Stadtmauer (*f.*)
to clear away, vacate räumen
climate Klima (*n.*)
clock; hour; watch Uhr (*f.*)
to close zumachen
clothes Kleider (*pl.*)
coach (athletic), trainer Trainer (*m.*)
coat Mantel (*m.*)
cock-and-bull story Ammenmärchen (*n.*)
coffee Kaffee (*m.*)
coke (Coca-Cola) Coca (*f.*), Cola (*f.*)
cold Erkältung (*f.*)
cold kalt
to collect sammeln
Cologne Köln
to come kommen
communist Kommunist (*m.*)
computer Computer (*m.*)
concert Konzert (*n.*)
conductor (transportation) Schaffner (*m.*)
conflict Konflikt (*m.*)
constitution Konstitution (*f.*)
continent Erdteil (*m.*)
to control kontrollieren
cool kühl
to copy kopieren
corn Mais (*m.*)
corner Ecke (*f.*)
count Graf (*m.*)

cow Kuh (*f.*)
to cry weinen
cupboard Schrank (*m.*)
to cut schneiden
to dance tanzen
dangerous gefährlich
dark dunkel
daughter Tochter (*f.*)
day Tag (*m.*)
death Tod (*m.*)
December Dezember (*m.*)
to delegate, send as a delegate delegieren
to demonstrate demonstrieren
Denmark Dänemark
dentist Zahnarzt (*m.*)
department store Kaufhaus (*n.*)
to describe beschreiben
desk Schreibtisch (*m.*)
dessert Nachtisch (*m.*)
to destroy zerstören
dialect Dialekt (*m.*)
dictionary Wörterbuch (*n.*)
difficult schwer
diligent fleißig
diplomat Diplomat (*m.*)
to dispatch absenden
to do tun
to do handicrafts basteln
door Tür (*f.*)
to drink trinken
to drive, travel fahren
drugstore Drogerie (*f.*)
duke Herzog (*m.*)
during während
each jeder
early früh
earth, Earth Erde (*f.*)
east Osten (*m.*)
easy leicht
eat essen
eat (used for animals) fressen
effective effektiv
eight acht
eighteen achtzehn
eighty achtzig
eleven elf
emperor Kaiser (*m.*)
empire Reich (*n.*)
entire, whole ganz
evening Abend (*m.*)
examination Examen (*n.*)
except außer
to expect, await erwarten
expensive teuer
to fall fallen
to fall in love sich verlieben
family Familie (*f.*)
far weit
farmer Bauer (*m.*)
to fascinate faszinieren

fast schnell

father Vater (*m.*)

February Februar (*m.*)

federal parliament Bundestag (*m.*)

to feel empfinden

to feel fühlen

fifteen fünfzehn

fifty fünfzig

to find finden

fir, pine tree Tanne (*f.*)

fish Fisch (*m.*)

to fit passen

five fünf

to flood überschwemmen

floor Boden (*m.*)

floor lamp Stehlampe (*f.*)

flower Blume (*f.*)

to fly fliegen

to follow folgen

fondly gern

food Essen (*n.*)

for für

foreigner Ausländer (*m.*)

to forget vergessen

forty vierzig

four vier

fourteen vierzehn

fox Fuchs (*m.*)

Friday Freitag (*m.*)

friend Freund (*m.*)

from, of von

from where woher

fruit Obst (*n.*)

fruit pie Obstkuchen (*m.*)

funny komisch

to gather, collect sammeln

German Deutsche (*m./f.*)

German champagne Sekt (*m.*)

Germanic germanisch

Germany Deutschland

get off (transportation) aussteigen

get on (transportation) einsteigen

gift Geschenk (*n.*)

girl Mädchen (*n.*)

girlfriend Freundin (*f.*)

to give geben

glass Glas (*n.*)

glove Handschuh (*m.*)

to go gehen

to go along mitgehen

to go cycling Rad fahren

to go in for, pursue; participate in; drive treiben

go skiing Ski laufen

God Gott (*m.*)

good gut

good-bye auf Wiederschauen, auf Wiedersehen

good day, hello guten Tag

good evening guten Abend

good morning guten Morgen
good night gute Nacht
government Regierung (*f.*)
grain Korn (*n.*)
grandchild Enkel (*m.*)
grandfather Großvater (*m.*)
grandmother Großmutter (*f.*)
grass Gras (*n.*)
gray grau
green grün
to greet grüßen
to grow wachsen
guest Gast (*m.*)
half halb
hallway Flur (*m.*)
ham Schinken (*m.*)
to hang hängen
to happen geschehen
to happen passieren
happy, lucky glücklich
harbor Hafen (*m.*)
harbor excursion Hafenrundfahrt (*f.*)
hare Hase (*m.*)
hat Hut (*m.*)
to have haben
to have the opinion, mean meinen
heads or tails Kopf oder Zahl
healthy gesund
to hear hören
heart Herz (*n.*)
heavy schwer
hedgehog Igel (*m.*)
hell Hölle (*f.*)
to help helfen
her ihr
here hier
high hoch
to hike, wander wandern
hippo Nilpferd (*n.*)
his sein
history Geschichte (*f.*)
hockey Eishockey (*n.*)
to hold halten
holy heilig
home(ward) nach Hause
to horrify entsetzen
horse Pferd (*n.*)
hospital Krankenhaus (*n.*)
hot heiß
hour Stunde (*f.*)
house Haus (*n.*)
how, as wie
human, person Mensch (*m.*)
hundred hundert
hungry hungrig
hunt Jagd (*f.*)
hurry sich beeilen
ice, ice cream Eis (*n.*)
if wenn
to imagine sich vorstellen

to imitate imitieren
to immigrate immigrieren
to impress imponieren
in in
to inform, notify mitteilen
insane wahnsinnig
in spite of trotz
instead of anstatt (statt)
to instruct, teach unterrichten
interesting interessant
to interrupt unterbrechen
to introduce vorstellen
to invite einladen
Italy Italien
jacket Jacke (*f.*)
January Januar (*m.*)
job Job (*m.*)
July Juli (*m.*)
June Juni (*m.*)
key Schlüssel (*m.*)
to kick, shove stoßen
king König (*m.*)
to kiss küssen
kitchen Küche (*f.*)
to knock klopfen
to know, be acquainted with kennen
to know wissen
lady Dame (*f.*)
lager beer Pils (*n.*)
lamp Lampe (*f.*)
landlady Wirtin (*f.*)
last letzte
late spät
to laugh lachen
law Jura (*n./pl.*)
lawn Rasen (*m.*)
lawyer Rechtsanwalt (*m.*)
to lay legen
leader Führer (*m.*)
to learn lernen
left link
less; minus weniger
to let lassen
library Bibliothek (*f.*)
to lie, recline lügen
to lie (omit the truth) lügen
light, easy leicht
light Licht (*n.*)
to like, please gefallen
little, small klein
little, few wenig
little bit bisschen
living room Wohnzimmer (*n.*)
long lang
to look at ansehen
to look for suchen
to look like aussehen
to lose verlieren
loud laut
to love lieben

main railroad station Hauptbahnhof (*m.*)
male nurse Pfleger (*m.*)
to manifest manifestieren
many, much viel(e)
to march marschieren
March März (*m.*)
market square Marktplatz (*m.*)
married verheiratet
May Mai (*m.*)
meat Fleisch (*n.*)
mechanic Mechaniker (*m.*)
merchant Kaufmann (*m.*)
milk Milch (*f.*)
million Million (*f.*)
mineral water Mineralwasser (*n.*)
minus minus
Monday Montag (*m.*)
monster Ungeheuer (*n.*)
month Monat (*m.*)
more mehr
morning Morgen (*m.*)
mother Mutter (*f.*)
motorcycle Motorrad (*n.*)
movie Film (*m.*)
movie theater Kino (*n.*)
Munich München
music Musik (*f.*)
my mein
name Name (*m.*)
to name nennen
nation Nation (*f.*)
near nah
to need brauchen
neighbor Nachbar (*m.*)
never nie
new neu
newspaper Zeitung (*f.*)
next to, near neben
nice nett
night Nacht (*f.*)
nine neun
nineteen neunzehn
ninety neunzig
no one niemand
north Norden (*m.*)
North America Nordamerika
not nicht
not any, none kein
to note, make a note of something notieren
notebook Heft (*n.*)
nothing nichts
novel Roman (*m.*)
November November (*m.*)
now jetzt
nurse Krankenschwester (*f.*)
nursery school teacher Erzieher (*m.*)
October Oktober (*m.*)
official, government employee Beamte (*m.*)
often oft
old alt

on auf
on foot zu Fuß
one eins
one man
to open aufmachen
opposite gegenüber
or oder
to order bestellen
to organize organisieren
our unser
out aus
outing Ausflug (*m.*)
oven Ofen (*m.*)
over, above über
package Paket (*n.*)
pain Schmerz (*m.*)
parents Eltern (*pl.*)
park Park (*m.*)
parliament Parlament (*n.*)
party Party (*f.*)
party (political) Partei (*f.*)
passport Pass (*m.*)
patient Kranke (*m.*)
peas Erbsen (*pl.*)
pencil Bleistift (*m.*)
people Leute (*pl.*)
people, nation Volk (*n.*)
person Mensch (*m.*)
pessimist Pessimist (*m.*)
pet Haustier (*n.*)
to photograph fotografieren
photographer Fotograf (*m.*)
physician Arzt (*m.*)
physicist Physiker (*m.*)
piano Klavier (*n.*)
picnic Picknick (*n.*)
picture Bild (*n.*)
picture postcard Ansichtskarte (*f.*)
pig Schwein (*n.*)
pilot Pilot (*m.*)
pink rosa
plant Pflanze (*f.*)
to plant pflanzen
to play spielen
please bitte
to please, make happy erfreuen
to pluck rupfen
plus plus
pocket Tasche (*f.*)
poet Dichter (*m.*)
police Polizei (*f.*)
polite höflich
politician Politiker (*m.*)
poor arm
position Position (*f.*)
to possess, own besitzen
postcard Postkarte (*f.*)
post office Post (*f.*)
postage stamp Briefmarke (*f.*)
poster Poster (*n.*)

potato Kartoffel (*f.*)
pregnant schwanger
prep school Gymnasium (*n.*)
president Präsident (*m.*)
pretty schön
probably wahrscheinlich
problem Problem (*n.*)
to produce produzieren
professor Professor (*m.*)
to program programmieren
to promise versprechen
to pronounce aussprechen
to protect schützen
to protest protestieren
to push schieben
to put, place stellen
quarter Viertel (*n.*)
queen Königin (*f.*)
rabbit Kaninchen (*n.*)
radio Radio (*n.*)
railroad station Bahnhof (*m.*)
rain Regen (*m.*)
to rain regnen
to read lesen
to receive bekommen
to recommend empfehlen
to recruit werben
red rot
to reflect widerspiegeln
to relate erzählen
relative Verwandte (*m.*)
to report berichten
republic Republik (*f.*)
to request bitten
to restore restaurieren
reunification Wiedervereinigung (*f.*)
rice Reis (*m.*)
to ride reiten
right recht
to rinse spülen
river Fluss (*m.*)
roast sausage Bratwurst (*f.*)
Roman römisch
room Zimmer (*n.*)
rose Rose (*f.*)
to run laufen, rennen
to run away weglaufen
Russian russisch
same derselbe
sandwich Butterbrot (*n.*)
Saturday Samstag, Sonnabend (*m.*)
to say sagen
schedule Fahrplan (*m.*)
school Schule (*f.*)
scientist Wissenschaftler (*m.*)
to scratch kratzen
season Jahreszeit (*f.*)
to seat oneself sich setzen
second zweite
secretary Sekretär (*m.*)

to see sehen
to sell verkaufen
to send schicken
to send senden
September September (*m.*)
to serve dienen
to set setzen
seven sieben
seventeen siebzehn
seventy siebzig
shall, will werden
to shave rasieren
sheep Schaf (*n.*)
ship Schiff (*n.*)
shop, store Laden (*m.*)
short kurz
to shout schreien
siblings Geschwister (*pl.*)
sick krank
sights Sehenswürdigkeiten (*pl.*)
sightseeing tour Besichtigung (*f.*)
since seit
to sing singen
singer Sänger (*m.*)
sister Schwester (*f.*)
to sit sitzen
six sechs
sixteen sechzehn
sixty sechzig
sky Himmel (*m.*)
to sleep schlafen
slow langsam
smart klug
to smoke rauchen
snake Schlange (*f.*)
snow Schnee (*m.*)
to snow schneien
soccer Fußball (*m.*)
soccer player Fußballspieler (*m.*)
sofa Sofa (*n.*)
someone jemand
son Sohn (*m.*)
song Lied (*n.*)
Sunday Sonntag (*m.*)
soon bald
south Süden (*m.*)
South America Südamerika
sparkling water Sprudel (*m.*)
sparkling wine Sekt (*m.*)
to speak sprechen
to speak to anreden
to spend ausgeben
to spoil, rot verderben
sport (form of) Sportart (*f.*)
spring Frühling (*m.*)
to stand stehen
to stand back, remain behind zurückbleiben
to start, begin anfangen
to stay, remain bleiben

to steal stehlen
stairs, staircase Treppe (*f.*)
still noch
story, history Geschichte (*f.*)
street Straße (*f.*)
streetcar Straßenbahn (*f.*)
to stroll spazieren
to study studieren
summer Sommer (*m.*)
Sunday Sonntag (*m.*)
supper Abendessen (*n.*)
to swear schwören
sweater Pullover (*m.*)
sweatshirt Sweatshirt (*n.*)
Sweden Schweden
to swim schwimmen
table Tisch (*m.*)
table tennis Tischtennis (*m.*)
to take along/with mitnehmen
to talk reden
taxi driver Taxifahrer (*m.*)
tea Tee (*m.*)
teacher Lehrer (*m.*)
telegram Telegramm (*n.*)
ten zehn
to thank danken
that dass (*conj.*)
that jener
there da, dort
there is/are es gibt
thief Dieb (*m.*)
to think denken
third dritte
thirst Durst (*m.*)
thirteen dreizehn
thirty dreißig
this dieser
thousand tausend
three drei
through durch
Thursday Donnerstag (*m.*)
ticket Fahrkarte (*f.*)
tiger Tiger (*m.*)
time Zeit (*f.*)
tired müde
to zu
today heute
today's (*adj.*) heutig
tomorrow morgen
tongue Zunge (*f.*)
too zu
tour Tour (*f.*)
tourist Tourist (*m.*)
to tow away abschleppen
traffic Verkehr (*m.*)
train Zug (*m.*)
to transfer umsteigen
to travel reisen
tree Baum (*m.*)
tribe Stamm (*m.*)

trillion Billion (*f.*)
trip Reise (*f.*)
to try probieren
Tuesday Dienstag (*m.*)
tulip Tulpe (*f.*)
tunnel Tunnel (*m.*)
twelve zwölf
twenty zwanzig
twins Zwillinge (*pl.*)
two zwei
umbrella Regenschirm (*m.*)
uncle Onkel (*m.*)
under unter
to understand verstehen
unfortunately leider
university Universität (*f.*)
until, as far as bis
vase Vase (*f.*)
vegetable soup Gemüsesuppe (*f.*)
vegetables Gemüse (*n.*)
very sehr
vicinity Nähe (*f.*)
Vienna Wien
village Dorf (*n.*)
violin Geige (*f.*)
to visit besuchen
to wait warten
wall Wand (*f.*)
war Krieg (*m.*)
warm warm
to wash waschen
water Wasser (*n.*)
to wear tragen
weather Wetter (*n.*)
Wednesday Mittwoch (*m.*)
week Woche (*f.*)
weekend Wochenende (*n.*)
west Westen (*m.*)
what was
when wann
whenever wenn
where wo
where to wohin
whether ob
which welcher
white weiß
who wer
whose wessen
why warum
wife, woman Frau (*f.*)
to win, gain gewinnen
window Fenster (*n.*)
wine Wein (*m.*)
wing Flügel (*m.*)
winter Winter (*m.*)
with mit
without ohne
wolf Wolf (*m.*)
woman, wife Frau (*f.*)
word Wort (*n.*)

to work arbeiten

worker Arbeiter (*m.*)

world war Weltkrieg (*m.*)

to write schreiben

writer Schriftsteller (*m.*)

year Jahr (*n.*)

yellow gelb

yesterday gestern

you du, ihr, Sie

young jung

your dein, euer, Ihr

zoo Zoo (*m.*)

ANSWER KEY

CHAPTER 1

Quiz

1. ss
2. ß
3. ß
4. ß
5. ss
6. long
7. long
8. long
9. short
10. short

CHAPTER 2

Written Practice 2-1

1. Wer ist das? Das ist Sabine.
2. Wer ist das? Das ist der Professor.
3. Was ist das? Das ist der Stuhl.
4. Was ist das? Das ist die Schule.
5. Wer ist das? Das ist das Kind.
6. Was ist das? Das ist das Haus.
7. Was ist das? Das ist die Lampe.
8. Wer ist das? Das ist Frau Benz.
9. Wer ist das? Das ist Angela.
10. Was ist das? Das ist der Wagen.

Written Practice 2-2

8 3 4 6 1 7 5 2

Quiz

1. b. Gut, danke.
2. a. Erik
3. c. Das ist die Bluse.
4. a. Nicht so gut.
5. c. Das ist der Tourist.
6. Was ist das? Das ist der Apfel.
7. Wer ist das? Das ist die Lehrerin.
8. Wer ist das? Das ist der Mann.
9. Guten Morgen.
10. Guten Abend.

CHAPTER 3

Written Practice 3-1

1. Geht er zum Stadtpark?
2. Geht Otto zur Schule?
3. Geht Astrid zur Party?
4. Geht sie zum Bahnhof?
5. Geht Herr Keller zur Arbeit?
6. Geht Frau Bauer zum Restaurant?
7. Geht das Kind zur Bibliothek?
8. Geht Professor Schneider nach Hause?

Written Practice 3-2

1. geht 2. wohnt/ist 3. ist 4. Wohnt 5. Ist 6. geht 7. ist 8. Ist 9. wohnt/ist 10. Geht

Written Practice 3-3

2 7 3 1 4 6 8 9 5

Quiz

1. c. Nein, in Hamburg.
2. a. Nein, es geht Astrid gut.

3. b. Nein, er geht zur Party.
4. a. Nein, in der Hauptstraße.
5. a. Nein, er geht nicht zur Bibliothek.
6. Geht das Kind zur Schule?
7. Geht das Mädchen zur Party?
8. Geht Frau Schneider zum Restaurant?
9. Geht er zur Bibliothek?
10. Geht der Tourist nach Hause?

CHAPTER 4

Written Practice 4-1

1. Wo 2. Wohin 3. Wo 4. Wohin 5. Wo

Written Practice 4-2

5 1 8 2 4 6 9 3 7

Quiz

1. b. Nein, er hat morgen eine Prüfung.
2. c. Ein Kleid.
3. a. Ein Hemd.
4. a. Nicht weit von hier.
5. a. Er reist nach Italien.
6. Renate hat eine Bluse.
7. Sie haben einen Hut.
8. Erik und Felix haben ein Problem.
9. Ich habe eine Lampe.
10. Ihr habt Socken und Schuhe.

CHAPTER 5

Written Practice 5-1

1. Wie viel ist vier plus fünf? Vier plus fünf ist neun.
2. Wie viel ist sieben minus drei? Sieben minus drei ist vier.
3. Wie viel ist zehn plus sechs? Zehn plus sechs ist sechzehn.

4. Wie viel ist zwanzig minus neun? Zwanzig minus neun ist elf.
5. Wie viel ist vierzig plus dreißig? Vierzig plus dreißig ist siebzig.
6. Wie viel ist neunzig minus fünfzig? Neunzig minus fünfzig ist vierzig.
7. Wie viel ist dreiunddreißig plus zwei? Dreiunddreißig plus zwei ist fünfunddreißig.
8. Wie viel ist achtzig minus einundvierzig? Achtzig minus einundvierzig ist neununddreißig.
9. Wie viel ist elf plus zwölf? Elf plus zwölf ist dreiundzwanzig.
10. Wie viel ist hundert minus neunundneunzig? Hundert minus neunundneunzig ist eins.

Written Practice 5-2

5 3 2 8 4 6 1 7

Quiz

1. b. Am Elften dieses Monats.
2. a. Nein, meine Bluse ist neu.
3. c. Dreiundsiebzig.
4. a. Am neunzehnten Februar.
5. a. Er ist alt.
6. Die Frau ist am elften Februar geboren.
7. Mein Sohn ist am dreiundzwanzigsten Juni geboren.
8. Dein Vater ist am dritten November geboren.
9. Meine Großmutter ist nicht alt. Sie ist jung.
10. Mein Bruder ist nicht alt. Er ist jung.

PART ONE TEST

1. c. Gut, danke.
2. c. Sabine.
3. c. Das ist die Jacke.
4. a. Das ist meine Mutter.
5. c. Nein, in Berlin.
6. a. Nein, es geht Sabine gut.
7. b. Nein, sie geht zur Party.

8. a. Eine Bluse.
9. c. Einen Hut.
10. a. In Frankreich.
11. c. Sie reist nach Österreich.
12. b. Am Elften dieses Monats.
13. a. Nein, es ist alt.
14. c. Achtundsechzig.
15. a. Am dritten Juni.
16. Wer ist das? Das ist die Lehrerin.
17. Was ist das? Das ist das Hemd.
18. Was ist das? Das ist die Lampe.
19. Guten Morgen.
20. Guten Tag.
21. Auf Wiedersehen.
22. Wohin geht Herr Keller?
23. Wo ist deine Tochter?
24. Frau Schäfer hat eine Bluse.
25. Ich habe ein Hemd.

CHAPTER 6

Written Practice 6-1

1. Wo ist der Bus? Jürgen sieht den Bus.
2. Wo ist die Jacke? Jürgen sieht die Jacke.
3. Wo ist der Bahnhof? Jürgen sieht den Bahnhof.
4. Wo ist der Wagen? Jürgen sieht den Wagen.
5. Wo ist die Brücke? Jürgen sieht die Brücke.
6. Wo sind die Handschuhe? Jürgen sieht die Handschuhe.
7. Wo ist der Flughafen? Jürgen sieht den Flughafen.
8. Wo ist das Museum? Jürgen sieht das Museum.
9. Wo ist das Kino? Jürgen sieht das Kino.
10. Wo ist die Bushaltestelle? Jürgen sieht die Bushaltestelle.

Written Practice 6-2

1. sieht 2. Siehst 3. sehe 4. findet 5. findet 6. findest

Written Practice 6-3

6 4 2 1 3 5

Quiz

1. b. Sie ist krank.
2. b. Er findet einen Hut.
3. c. Ja, sie hat ihn gern.
4. a. Ich weiß nicht. Ich sehe es nicht.
5. c. Nein, ich werde ihn zum Arzt bringen.
6. Ich sehe ein Museum.
7. Ich sehe einen Bahnhof.
8. Ich sehe einen Zug.
9. Ich sehe eine Brücke.
10. Ich sehe ein Flugzeug.

CHAPTER 7

Written Practice 7-1

1. Nein, ich trinke lieber Wein.
2. Nein, er trinkt lieber Wasser.
3. Nein, sie trinkt lieber Kaffee.
4. Nein, ich esse lieber Fisch.
5. Nein, er isst lieber Steak.
6. Nein, ich esse lieber Salat.
7. Nein, wir essen lieber Suppe.
8. Nein, sie isst lieber Obst.
9. Nein, ich esse lieber Eis.
10. Nein, ich esse lieber Schweinefleisch.
11. Nein, ich esse lieber Butter.
12. Nein, ich trinke lieber Milch.

Written Practice 7-2

1. gehört 2. bestellt 3. gelesen 4. gereist 5. gebraucht

Written Practice 7-3

7 2 4 1 5 8 3 6

Quiz

1. c. Ja, ich habe Hunger.
2. b. Ich habe Erdbeeren mit Schlagsahne bestellt.
3. c. Milch.
4. c. Im Restaurant.
5. a. Die Speisekarte.
6. Ich habe Suppe bestellt.
7. Ich habe Eis bestellt.
8. Ich habe Tee bestellt.
9. Ich habe Kartoffeln bestellt.
10. Ich habe Obst bestellt.

CHAPTER 8

Written Practice 8-1

1. Sie hat meine Bluse an.
2. Ich trage sein rotes Hemd.
3. Sabine kauft euren Wagen.
4. Verkaufst du deine Ohrringe?
5. Verkaufen Sie Ihren Rock?
6. Sein Anzug gefällt mir sehr.
7. Unsere Lehrerin ist zu Hause.
8. Ihr Kleid ist sehr teuer.
9. Er wird meinen VW kaufen.
10. Sie trägt seine Jacke.

Written Practice 8-2

1. Meine 2. Unsere 3. Ihr 4. Seine 5. dein

Written Practice 8-3

3 6 4 1 8 2 5 7

Quiz

1. b. Vierzig Euro.
2. a. Ein rotes Kleid.

3. c. Sie verkaufen ihren Wagen.
4. a. Nein, das ist meine neue Windjacke.
5. b. Sie trägt schwarze Stiefel.
6. Erik hat einen Badeanzug gekauft.
7. Erik hat Ohrringe gekauft.
8. Erik hat Sandalen gekauft.
9. Erik hat einen Regenmantel gekauft.
10. Erik hat eine Armbanduhr gekauft.

CHAPTER 9

Written Practice 9-1

1. billiger 2. älter 3. schöner 4. schneller 5. besser

Written Practice 9-2

6 4 2 3 5 1 8 7

Quiz

1. a. Es ist halb neun. Mach schnell!
2. c. Nein, er ist sehr leicht.
3. b. Nein, sprechen Sie bitte Englisch!
4. a. Nein, ich möchte lieber einen Salat.
5. a. Ja, Sabine ist jünger als Thomas.
6. Ich habe den Zoo besucht.
7. Ich habe die Universität besucht.
8. Ich habe die Stadt besucht.
9. Ich habe den Hafen besucht.
10. Ich habe das Dorf besucht.

CHAPTER 10

Written Practice 10-1

1. In den Bergen.
2. Am Strand.
3. Im Wald./In den Bergen.

4. In der Stadt.
5. In der Stadt.
6. In den Bergen.
7. Am Strand.
8. Am Strand.
9. Am Strand./In der Stadt./Im Wald.
10. Im Wald./In den Bergen.

Written Practice 10-2

1. am billigsten 2. am ältesten 3. am größten 4. am kleinsten
5. am besten

Written Practice 10-3

5 2 8 6 4 7 3 1

Quiz

1. b. Es regnet wieder.
2. a. Nein, mit dem Zug.
3. c. Ja, und es ist sehr kalt.
4. c. Im Wald.
5. c. Sonnenbaden.
6. Im Juli ist es heiß.
7. Im Oktober ist es windig.
8. Im April ist es regnerisch.
9. Im November ist es kühl.
10. Im Mai ist es neblig.

PART TWO TEST

1. b. Er ist krank.
2. c. Ja, er hat sie gern.
3. a. Ich weiß nicht. Ich sehe es nicht.
4. c. Ja, ich habe Hunger.
5. a. Kaffee
6. c. Im Restaurant.
7. b. Fünfzig Euro.

8. a. Ein grünes Kleid.
9. c. Er trägt ein weißes Sweatshirt.
10. a. Es ist halb zehn.
11. b. Nein, sprechen Sie bitte Englisch!
12. b. Nein, sein Bruder ist älter.
13. b. Es regnet wieder.
14. a. Nein, im Sommer ist es heiß.
15. c. Am Strand.
16. Erik sieht das Museum.
17. Erik sieht den Bahnhof.
18. Erik sieht den Arzt.
19. Erik sieht die Brücke.
20. Erik sieht die Stiefel.
21. Ich trinke keine Milch.
22. Ich trinke keinen Tee.
23. Ich esse kein Obst.
24. Ich esse keine Eier.
25. Ich trinke keinen Kaffee.

CHAPTER 11

Written Practice 11-1

1. Brittas Mutter ist großzügig.
2. Tinas Onkel ist großzügig.
3. Werners Bruder ist großzügig.
4. Andreas Schwester ist großzügig.
5. Ralfs Freundin ist großzügig.
6. Gabis Verlobter ist großzügig.
7. Stefans Arzt ist großzügig.
8. Angelas Kinder sind großzügig.
9. Christophs Tochter ist großzügig.
10. Sonjas Eltern sind großzügig.

Written Practice 11-2

1. dem Mann 2. dir 3. seiner Schwester 4. Ihnen 5. den Kindern

Written Practice 11-3

5 3 4 2 7 8 1 6

Quiz

1. c. Sabines Sohn.
2. a. Die Tochter meines Bruders schläft noch.
3. b. Einem Freund.
4. c. Ich möchte einen dunkelblauen Pulli.
5. a. Sie geben uns das Geld.
6. Ich gebe Werner den Brief.
7. Ich gebe deiner Frau die Rose.
8. Ich gebe den Kindern ein Buch.
9. Ich gebe dir ein Geschenk.
10. Ich gebe dem Professor die Handschuhe.

CHAPTER 12

Written Practice 12-1

1. Nein, diese Einladung ist für sie.
2. Nein, diese Einladung ist für dich.
3. Nein, diese Einladung ist für Sie.
4. Nein, diese Einladung ist für meinen Professor.
5. Nein, diese Einladung ist für die Ärztin.
6. Nein, diese Einladung ist für uns.
7. Nein, diese Einladung ist für euch.
8. Nein, diese Einladung ist für mich.
9. Nein, diese Einladung ist für meine Cousine.
10. Nein, diese Einladung ist für meinen Bruder.

Written Practice 12-2

1. für 2. bei 3. ohne 4. aus 5. mit

Written Practice 12-3

8 5 2 1 7 4 6 3

Quiz

1. b. Die Einladung ist für dich.
2. a. Hier vermietet man Wagen.
3. c. Vier Stunden.
4. c. Der Zug nach Darmstadt.
5. a. Ich muss mit dem Chef sprechen.
6. Seine Eltern arbeiten für den Lehrer.
7. Ich arbeite für seinen Onkel.
8. Du arbeitest für ihre Tante.
9. Herr Benz arbeitet für uns.
10. Meine Tochter arbeitet für sie.

CHAPTER 13

Written Practice 13-1

1. arbeitete 2. warst 3. hatte 4. machte 5. gingen

Written Practice 13-2

5 3 2 8 6 4 7 1

Quiz

1. a. Morgen früh.
2. c. Eine Sinfonie von Mozart.
3. b. Sehr gut.
4. c. Ja, ich tanze gern aber nicht gut.
5. c. Nein, sie hört lieber Jazzmusik.
6. Der Richter war in der Kunstgallerie.
7. Der Richter hatte die Künstlerin gern.
8. Der Richter wohnte in der Stadt.
9. Der Richter spielte mit den Kindern.
10. Der Richter machte das Fenster auf.

CHAPTER 14

Written Practice 14-1

1. sich 2. dich 3. mich 4. uns 5. sich

Written Practice 14-2

6 2 4 8 3 5 7 1

Quiz

1. b. Nein, er ist im Wohnzimmer.
2. b. Er ist im Juni gestorben.
3. c. Nein, aufs Bett.
4. a. Zwischen dem Sessel und dem Schrank.
5. c. Im Schlafzimmer haben wir einen Schreibtisch und ein Bett.
6. In der Küche gibt es einen Herd.
7. Im Schlafzimmer gibt es einen Schreibtisch.
8. Im Esszimmer gibt es vier Stühle.
9. Im Flur gibt es einen Kleiderschrank.
10. Im Keller gibt es einen Kühlschrank.

CHAPTER 15

Written Practice 15-1

1. darauf 2. neben ihm 3. daran 4. darüber 5. auf sie

Written Practice 15-2

7 3 2 4 1 8 5 6

Quiz

1. b. Nein, zwei Zeitschriften.
2. b. Eine neue Kindersendung.
3. c. Im dritten Programm.
4. c. Einen Krimi.
5. a. Nein, sie fährt nie damit.
6. Heute gibt es eine Übertragung eines Tennisspiels.
7. Heute gibt es eine Übertragung einer Oper.
8. Heute gibt es eine Übertragung des Fußballspiels.

9. Heute gibt es eine Übertragung des Balletts.
10. Heute gibt es eine Übertragung einer Sinfonie von Brahms.

FINAL TEST

1. c. Sabines Sohn.
2. a. Der Sohn des Richters schläft noch.
3. c. Einem Freund.
4. c. Ich möchte ein rotes Hemd.
5. a. Ein Bus.
6. c. Wir möchten mit dem Chef sprechen.
7. c. Nächsten Montag.
8. c. Eine Sinfonie von Beethoven.
9. c. Ausgezeichnet.
10. b. Nein, es liegt noch auf dem Bett.
11. c. Nein, ich habe nicht davon gesprochen.
12. b. Eine neue Sportsendung.
13. c. Im ersten Programm.
14. b. Gestern nachmittag.
15. c. Da haben wir ein Sofa und einen Sessel.
16. Tina fotografiert das Museum.
17. Tina fotografiert den Bahhof.
18. Tina fotografiert den Arzt/die Ärztin.
19. Tina fotografiert die Wohnung.
20. Tina fotografiert den Schauspieler.
21. Niemand war in der Kunstgallerie.
22. Niemand hatte seinen Freund gern.
23. Niemand wohnte in dieser Wohnung.
24. Niemand wartete darauf.
25. Niemand machte die Tür auf.

INDEX